Oregon Days

A Compilation of Youthful Adventures of an Oregon Boy

Written by

Christopher Sage

and Illustrated by
Alison Paolini

Credits and Copyrights-

ISBN-13: 978-1519767202
ISBN-10: 151976720X

Dedication

I dedicate this book to the memory of my loving Grandparents whose hallowed care, faithful understanding and blessed patience, enabled me to grow and achieve.

Contents

Carolyn:

At long last — please take this
Book as a token of my respect and
Admiration...

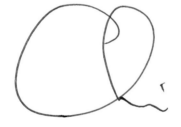

Acknowledgements

I would like to acknowledge Tom Watson, Allison Paolini and The Paradise Writers Group for their contributing faith and encouragement to this work. Each of these brilliant sources consistently encouraged me and I couldn't have produced this piece without their indispensible help.

Tom was a keen and timely resource concerning the publishing process. He continually provided me with timesaving and useful information at the most opportune time. I cannot thank this kind and knowledgeable American born Scots gentleman enough.

Allison was the lady I chose to create my illustrations. Her drawings were usually completed in just a few seconds yet I was continually amazed at how quickly my friend organized those lines of ink into a work of art. Allison completely captured the essence of each chapter quickly, precisely and in a delightful manner. My friend's profound artistic skill, perception and humanity impress me greatly every time I gaze at those quickly drawn but everlastingly meaningful sketches.

The Paradise Writers Group was also indispensible in their support of this piece. Those patient and kind people suffered through my book chapter by chapter as I read them through my editing process. Their encouragement and meaningful criticisms were always positive and I cannot thank them enough for their understanding and support.

Thank you all, I could not have succeeded without you.

Introduction

The setting for my narrative is rural southern Oregon in the mid nineteen fifties. Times were good, yet conditions primitive, with party lines, unpaved roads, lampless streets and distant hospitals being the norm. Family design was old fashioned, where strict fathers sanctioned and caring mothers loved. Almost everyone was employed in the timber industry or agriculture, making this pastoral locale a wonderful place to grow learn and experience life.

Medford, though diminutive, was a wonderful country hamlet. Big city issues such as large scale crime and litter was nonexistent. Medfordites took pride in their town and they had an interest in the well being of their neighbors. The schools were well administered with a high quality education being their consistent product. Hospitals were few and far between. However, neighborly interest and homestead first aid more than compensated for a shortage of professional help.

Our neighborhood was magnificent. Everyone respected one another and coexisted in a culture of rewarding hard work and strong family values. Each family knew every other family and all were bonded due to the common interests associated with a wonderful rural existence

Chapter 1
My Grandparents

My grandparents were magnificent folks. They had their faults, yet they were the only people who loved me, and looked after me for most of my young life.

They assumed the roles of my parents after I was abandoned by my mother and were always there for me, never faltering in their adopted responsibilities. Patient, level headed Christian countenance was the hallmark approach they utilized in rearing me. I will forever be indebted to them both and I miss them dearly.

The matriarch of my family was a short buxom lady with a curvaceous physique. She was always appropriately dressed and was never seen without a color coordinated apron or her high heels. My grandmother was exceptionally clean and continuously kept her hair and nails well manicured.

I will forever recall the perpetual aroma of sweet perfume that softly announced my gramma's presence.

My grandmother was born in Glasgow, Scotland, around the turn of the last century. She often would tell me wonderful stories of Scotland and her substantial upbringing as the daughter of one of the towns bake shop owners. As a young girl she witnessed the Titanic sail in the vicinity of her home town as the majestic liner followed its notorious course to the north Atlantic. My grandmother was very happy growing up in her Scottish surroundings and didn't like the idea of leaving her Celtic homeland.

Gramma moved to the United States at the age of ten when my great grandfather decided to establish himself in Portland Oregon. The dramatic move turned out to be for the best, and my grandmother remained a baker's daughter until she met and wed my grampa following World War I. My gramma remained as the loving wife of my grampa for over fifty years until her unfortunate death in the fall of 1973.

If my grandmother had a fault, it was that she was too old fashioned. She firmly believed a woman's place was in the home. To some this viewpoint may seem archaic, but I believe her philosophy of life gave me a loving and solid foundation from which to grow and prosper.

My gramma was a wonderful woman. She was polite to all, God fearing, an outstanding cook, an excellent housekeeper and an extraordinary baker. She took exceptionally good care of me, seeing to my every need. I will always consider her as my mother.

My grandmother was popular as well as respected by everybody in our town. Every woman in our neighborhood loved her and continually sought her company. I never heard her raise her voice or swear and she always saw the positive side of everyone she met. If a tense situation warranted her input, she would respond in a firm but reserved manner.

When I acted out and discipline was required, my gramma calmly approached the problem, never losing her composure.

She would dissect the situation, find a solution and fairly administer punishment. My grandmother never spanked me and I always valued her judgments as final.

Gramma was a Christian woman and made sure both my grandfather and I regularly attended church. She contributed enormously to Christian charities by continually knitting, crocheting and making crafting items for the gift shop of the local Providence Hospital Guild. Often she recruited me to assist in her charitable tasks. When I was idle, and complaining of having nothing to do, my grumbling was usually met with her standard reply, "Idle hands are the devil's workshop."

I really didn't mind helping my gramma as I always enjoyed spending time with that loving, saintly woman.

My grandmother was an exceptional cook. Her skill in the kitchen was best evidenced by the numerous neighborhood events she hosted. Christmas week, Easter week, Memorial Day and the Fourth of July, were holidays my gramma eagerly celebrated with all the people living close by.

3

Everything was provided at these events except alcohol. Ham, roast beef, turkey, along with multiple salads and desserts, were all cooked and served by my grandmother in buffet style. The food was delicious and no comfort was spared our guests.

Christmas and Easter were special celebrations. Stereophonic music was provided and the banquets lasted a full week. Everyone came to share their joy, and there were never any issues. It wasn't uncommon to see twenty people regularly attending these festivities. My gramma's holiday celebrations were loved by all as wholesome feasts of happiness.

Another of my grandmother's talents was baking. She learned the craft of baking from her father and she baked a wide variety of items for our family and the neighborhood.

Gramma was often asked to bake a wedding cake, birthday cake or other confection for one of our neighbors. She always obliged, never charging for her services. I'll forever recall the beauty of her cakes and her skill in fashioning cherubs, animals, infants, roses, or other figures from royal frosting.

At the table, I couldn't wait to finish my dinner to see what was for dessert. Cakes, pies, pastries and cookies were abundant around our home. They always tasted better than the store bought items and were decorated to perfection.

I ceaselessly enjoyed examining the decorations of her baked goods. It was kind of a game my grandmother and I played with each other.

I recall a birthday cake gramma made for me. Every member of my grade school football team was represented in great detail. The faces, physical features, colors of the uniforms, and jersey numbers, of every player matched those of the real life counterpart. That cake was a real work of art, and must have taken her days of careful and secret labor to complete. Gramma never failed to astound me with her baked creations and their memory still please me to this day.

Sometimes, I would help gramma bake an item. She would patiently show me how to mix, sift, or knead something, while I sufficiently coated myself with flour, frosting, or dough.

Ultimately, it didn't matter how messy I got as I was with my gramma, and loving every minute of it.

My Grandmother kept an extremely clean house, an outstanding feat when one considers the numerous celebrations she hosted while contending with a rambunctious young boy and his impish friends. Her house was always spotless and no amount of guests, celebrations, or dirty boys ever altered that fact. My friends and I were always running through her living room after playing in dirt or mud. We would soil her floors, carpet, and furnishings, then abruptly leave for another adventure. We were filthy little pigs, yet, my grandmother managed to keep our home as neat as a pin. What's more, she kept me scrubbed and cleaned, by sentencing me to the bathtub and supervising my hygiene on a daily basis. Gramma's concern for our family's cleanliness reflected the love she held for my grandfather as well as myself, and remains indelible in my memory to this day.

The care my Grandmother gave me can best be illustrated in the many loving favors she granted in return for good conduct. My grandmother was no pushover and I was rewarded only if I was well behaved. Often these rewards took the form of excursions. She wanted me to experience life in a positive way and a trip to Crater Lake, the Oregon Caves or going to a drive-in movie, were a few examples of the constructive diversions my gramma utilized to reward my good conduct.

I am still amazed by the memory of my grandmother regularly undertaking the task of supervising a group of young boys in venues such as a drive-in movie. Here, a woman in her late fifties would regularly sit in a station wagon with five to ten young hyperactive boys and watch a mind numbing horror movie as reward for my good manners. She was great, we always had fun, and everyone was polite and obedient, or we were on the road home.

My Grandmother's serene memory fills my heart with joy and admiration to this day. Her old fashioned ways may seem antiquated as compared to the views of the modern woman, but politeness and the value she placed on gracious living, remain in my memory as symbols of the good life. Gramma's belief in Christianity was a canon I recall with joyous happiness and remains fundamental to my philosophy of life. Her cooking, baking and domestic excellence fill my heart with the precious sense of home I hold so dear.

The selfless love and care she gave me was boundless and remains precious within my memory. I miss my grandmother and her deep adoration for me. I still mourn her passing greatly.

My grandfather was slightly taller than my grandmother. He had a stocky build, was bowlegged and possessed a full head of hair. My grampa was always clean-shaven and his weathered face housed two tender yet purposeful eyes. I remember him as continually being neatly dressed in khaki work clothing which included a shirt pocket full of pens and pencils. Grampa always carried a pocket knife that contained a host of attached gadgets which he called his pocket tool chest. My grandfather always had a cigarette in his hand and was never far from my Grandmother when he wasn't on a job.

The first twenty years of my grandfather's life were arduous and began when he was born on a southeastern Montana cattle ranch. His mother died giving him birth and his father passed away when he was the age of nine. Grampa was expected to pull his weight around the ranch while attending to his own meals and care at a very early age. After my great grandfather died, the ranch fell into the hands of my grandfather's eldest brother, who immediately evicted the rest of the family from the property. Grampa was on his own, riding the rails, working carnivals, and getting by as best he could. Fortunately, he grew up and survived World War I as an army mechanic.

After the war, my Grandfather utilized his talents in the peacetime economy working on cars and trucks.

He married my grandmother and after a short time passed, they settled in rural southern Oregon to raise their family through the roaring twenties as well as the great depression.

At the dawn of World War II, my grandfather joined the United States Navy. He survived that terrible conflict serving in Hawaii. He played a role in repairing and maintaining the victorious United States Pacific Fleet while stationed at the base in Honolulu.

Grampa felt fortunate to survive those two global conflicts, and was very proud of his wartime labors. Yet he rarely reminisced about his military service, preferring to discuss fishing or matters pertaining to his Christian family.

After the, Second World War, my grandfather returned to my grandmother and continued his career as a diesel mechanic.

He worked hard to provide for his family and steadily improved their standard of living. By the time I came along, grampa owned his own truck stop and was making a substantial living.

I had a large house to live in, forty plus acres to enjoy, and lots of animals to play with. Life was good and I felt blessed to dwell in the wholesome environment my grandfather made available.

Like everyone else, my grandfather had his faults. He was, by today's standards, an alcoholic and a chain smoker. However, he was never abusive or missed a day of work and was always available when needed.

If anything, he was my patriarch, and someone I could always turn to.

My grandfather was highly skilled in his chosen craft. He was regarded as the premier diesel technician in our area. Grampa possessed the ability to correctly diagnose as well as repair the countless mechanical problems our local loggers or farmers had with their vehicles and power units quickly and efficiently. Moreover, it was not uncommon for him to be called out of the area or out of state if someone was having mechanical difficulties with a truck, generator or tractor. Grampa was the faithful father figure I cherished. He was always available to patiently assist me with school projects, a difficult math problem or some confounding childhood issue.

Like me, my grandfather was abandoned at an early age. I feel this unfortunate similarity in the history of our two lives explains the deep understanding and love we shared. We each appreciated our family and our household in a very special way in addition to loving the life we shared together.

Grampa's calm and reserved approach to life was akin to my Gramma's. He never swore or raised his voice, and only spoke after long deliberation, considering his words well.

When I misbehaved, he always chose to hear my side of the story first. He unerringly could tell if I stretched the truth, and with the wisdom of Solomon, justly administered punishment without the need for spanking. I always accepted my grandfather's judgments as final and as was the case with my grandmother, I never argued with his loving concern for me.

My grampa was a devoted Christian husband and an unwavering foundation for our family. He loved my grandmother infinitely and always respected her wishes.

Grampa was ceaselessly available for my gramma and she never wanted for anything. I'll forever remember him as the compassionate, and loving, spouse to my grandmother and the leader of our family.

My grandfather was a highly respected leader in our community. He served on several steering committees for local organizations such as Kiwanis, the Chamber of Commerce and our Church. Grampa was forever involved in some fund raiser, charity drive or project designed to improve the area we lived in. Everyone in our area knew him as the "Go to person," to not only get a project started but finished and on time.

My grandfather was the finest man I have ever known. He had the toughest childhood, pre-adolescent and adolescent life I am aware of yet he had a limitless sense of benevolence and was kind to all. Grampa was a hard working, highly skilled benefactor, a warm and devoted paternal figure, a loyal and loving Christian husband, as well as a highly regarded member of our community.

I'll never forget my grandfather as the soft spoken, Christian leader of my family. Grampa loved and cared for me and my gramma profoundly. He eternally protected, provided and nurtured both my grandmother and myself. His selfless, affectionate guidance and understanding was invaluable to me and led to a level of love we shared until his tragic death in the spring of 1974.

My grandparents remain the two most precious people of my life. They unselfishly took me in without question and raised me in a loving Christian environment. They never failed me and were ceaselessly available whenever I stumbled on life's path. All I have become I owe to those two departed and angelic people.

Chapter 2

My Friends

We were a rowdy group numbering ten pre-adolescent boys. We never stole or vandalized property and we continually sought adventure within the bucolic splendor of our surroundings. The wonderful relationships I shared with; Adam, Harry, Jimmy, Reuben, Seth, Duane, Spencer, Heath, and Matt remain brilliant in my memory, never to fade.

Adam was my closest comrade. He lived next door and our personalities clicked from the moment we first met. Adam was tall, gaunt, and ambled with an unusual motion. This stride, coupled with his odd appearance, continually supplied our group with a source of mockery. Yet, Adam never lost his temper and always accepted his lampoonery with quiet reserve.

Ultimately, his calm and even tempered character was beneficial to our band as a constant source of wisdom.

Harry was the next childhood friend I fondly recall. He was the oldest of our group and the one we all admired. He was patient, kind and always willing to help fix our bikes, untangle a fishing reel, or solve a thousand other problems young boys seem to endlessly get themselves into. Harry was also our scientific inspiration. He was always tinkering with his chemistry set and amazing the rest of our troop with his mastery of the elements. Aeronautics was another scientific discipline familiar to Harry. We often marveled at the well crafted model aircraft he constructed. These planes really flew and were powered by miniature internal combustion engines. Adam, Jimmy, and I built model aircraft after Harry's example and they all flew due to our mentor's help and inspiration.

Another of my treasured boyhood buddies was Jimmy. Jimmy, the shortest member of our crowd, was mischievous and possessed the opposite personality of his older brother Harry. He continually concocted schemes we appreciated, and usually resulted in trouble of some kind. If an adventure was dangerous, or forbidden, Jimmy had a way of making it sound like fun with neither punishment nor injury being a consequence. Thankfully, we usually were dissuaded from Jimmy's impish influence via Adam's sound judgments.

The largest member of our clan was Reuben who easily dwarfed the rest of us by two feet in height and fifty pounds in weight. Generally, Reuben was a quiet giant and a good athlete.

He got along with everyone and exempting his size, fit in well with the other members of our squad. Reuben was our heavy lift person and vital to the cause if a sports contest was started or a task requiring strength was at hand. Later in life, Reuben's athletic prowess and enormous size earned him a football scholarship to a major university.

Seth was the second oldest member of our troop. Seth was the older brother of Reuben and usually content to go with the flow of the group. Seth wasn't outspoken unless the subject was fishing whereby he was transformed into a walking fountain of information and enthusiasm.

He became interested in fishing at an early age and like me, soon became a proficient angler with the assistance of his grandfather.

Seth had a God given feel for fishing and usually caught fish when the rest of us failed. His priceless knowledge of angling benefited every member of our pack when a fishing trip was on the agenda. To this day, I often utilize the numerous fishing tips Seth shared with me so long go.

Duane was the lead hunter and sports team captain of our party. Like Seth, he was an older brother and learned to stalk and slay quarry at an early age. He loved guns and continually practiced his aim earning the nickname of "Hawkeye" after the hero of James Fenimore Cooper's classic tales. Duane cherished hunting and his proficiency at tracking was remarkable. I was repeatedly amazed by his ability to discern the whereabouts of game via the slightest imprint in dirt or scratch on a rock. Duane was also an excellent athlete talented in football, basketball

and track. He was a natural leader and adept in devising strategies to win athletic contests. In football, he played the position of quarterback and his accurate passes won many games. Hawkeye also played point guard on the basketball team and scored a lot of points by utilizing his sharp eye for the rim. His outstanding stamina was advantageous in the sport of track and field. It seemed he could run forever, and he usually won the long distance events with ease. Ultimately, Hawkeye's athletic prowess and hunting competence suited him well and placed him as one of our group's leaders.

Spencer was the youngest member of our horde and the little brother of Duane. Spencer was the quintessential tag along. He pestered everyone endlessly with childish questions and needs. Conversely, everyone continually ridiculed Spencer and devised ways to escape his presence. Yet, he stuck with it and always managed to keep up with "the guys." In the end, we each liked having Spencer along.

We were concerned for his safety and always protected him from those who would take advantage of his lovable and toady nature.

Heath was the aquatic member of our troop. Heath and I had identical birth dates and we both loved to go to the local pool every summer.

Heath cherished swimming and developed into an excellent swimmer. He always was looking for a place to go for a dip during those hot Southern Oregon summer afternoons. It didn't matter if a body of water was a river, a lake, a stream or a public pool, the oases my friend sought only needed to be deep enough to wade for Heath to attempt a swim.

Heath's experiences in the water were not always fun filled. I recall one incident when he saved a boy from drowning.

We were playing in the shallow end of the local public pool when suddenly a boy from across town dove in and struck his head on the bottom. Heath immediately went into action.

He dove to the bottom, brought the unconscious boy to the surface and delivered him to the lifeguard while the rest of us looked on in wonder.

The lifeguard thanked Heath and later said, "He was very brave, as well as being responsible for saving the boy's life."

Heath was a true hero who made the front page of our local newspaper. We all were proud of him and bragged about his heroic exploits throughout that bygone summer.

Matt was the last of my childhood friends. Physically, Matt was obese. Psychologically, he was what is now described as bi-polar. Unfortunately, this curious profile caused him to be regarded as comical and something resembling Oliver Hardy of Laurel and Hardy films.

Matt had a terrible temper and was easily provoked from his relaxed character into torrid rages via the slightest annoyance. This malady, coupled with his overweight appearance, made him a target of humiliation by the rest of our band.

We often goaded Matt to anger by insulting him and then ran off to a safe distance to witness the disastrous carnage. He would swear and scream as he vented his wrath on some inanimate object while we chuckled at the spectacle before us.

Nevertheless, Matt was our friend and we each loyally appreciated him as a member of our posse.

Each of my boyhood friends were wonderful and vital contributors to the fantastic experiences I had as a young boy.

Their personalities, abilities, and varied interests gave me an unforgettable perspective of life as we explored the tranquil beauty of that long gone and treasured, rural environment.

Chapter 3

My Pets

I always will cherish the memories associated with the wonderful pets of my boyhood past. I remember Butch, Puck, Guildy, Tammy, Oliver, Narcissus, Smokey, Romeo, Hannibal, and Sammy as very different animals possessing varied dispositions. However, our pets were unified in one aspect, their appreciation for being part of our family.

Those fantastic pets each played a different yet consistent role in my life and gave me a profound sense of home still bright in my mind.

Butch was my first pet. He was a magnificent Labrador retriever and always at my side. He protected me without fail and never wavered in his loyalty. If I was troubled, he was always available to lick and comfort me.

Butch helped me to learn to take my first steps by continually sticking to my side to brace me and offering his loving assistance when I fell.

Butch and I had many adventures and I can still recall his first encounter with the rabbits in my grandfather's pasture.

My lab was a fairly fast dog but no match for the hare he came upon one summer morning. After rising and eating our respective breakfasts, we were off to attend to our daily duties. I was feeding the chickens and watching Butch as he policed the pasture behind our house. Romeo, our resident bull, was on the far side of the grazing land, thereby leaving Butch allowance to carry out his patrol unimpeded. Immediately, Butch confronted a bounding jackrabbit. He gave chase, but was no match for the hare's speed. After a few strides, Butch just stopped and stared with wonder at the speed exhibited by his lost quarry. I'll always remember the puzzled look on his face as he watched that rabbit spring away into the distance.

Puck was another cherished pet I remember from my boyhood past. Puck was a green parakeet named after the Shakespearian character from A Midsummer Night's Dream.

I still recall his friendly morning chirps greeting our family at breakfast.

Puck was a real character and was the master of several tricks. He loved beer and my grandfather taught Puck to perch on the rim of his stein so they could sip their brew together.

Another of Puck's tricks was nesting in my grandmother's hair.

He would fly to my grandmother's head, and begin fluffing her hair around him by scratching her scalp with his feet in a manner similar to the way a chicken scratches for food. Another of Puck's behaviors was his passion for the placement of his possessions.

These were the toys we purchased for him at the pet store.

Each toy was arranged personally by Puck on the shelf we constructed as his play area, never to be disturbed.

If a toy was placed out of order, Puck would drag it to the edge of his shelf and drop it to the floor.

A toy could only remain as one of his possessions if it was placed on its proper station within his play area.

Puck's character, tricks and behavior were hilarious and reminders of how such a tiny creature can give a family such a huge amount of joy. I'll never forget my little friend Puck.

Guildy was a Daschund and the second dog in my life. His given name was, Guildenstern, which translated from German meant Golden Star. Guildy was a very large dachshund with the torso the size of a standard sized retriever. Guildy was an exceptionally credentialed doxey, as his father was seven times best of breed champion. Nevertheless, Guildy's heritage didn't matter to our family – he was rescued from the pound, and we loved him for his character and not his papers.

Guildy had a wonderful disposition. He was intelligent, obedient, and loyal, and he had what we interpreted as a sense of humor. These traits endeared him to every member of our family. We still tell and retell stories of Guildy's exploits at family gatherings to this day.

Guildy was exceptionally intelligent and dutiful. He rarely misbehaved and would often survey a situation before becoming involved in some resultant punishment.

I recall one episode involving Guildy and Butch. Both dogs were off on one of their early morning patrols and were perilously close to an off limits area, the hen house. As they approached the outlawed area, I watched Guildy yelping and nipping at Butch's legs, while gazing back to me with the most worried expression on his face. At last he stopped and barked as Butch proceeded into the unguarded hen house. I still truly feel Guildy was attempting to stop Butch from getting into mischief and barking to get assistance toward rescuing his troubled canine friend.

Guildy was a very obedient dog. As a rule you only had to give him a command once. He would not repeat a forbidden act nor forget a command to either do or not do something.

Our doxey used to love to dig for gophers and was very successful at catching them. One day, early in his life, he was busy digging for his quarry in my grandmother's rose garden.

This was an absolute no no, and Guildy was promptly reprimanded for his misdeed. He never again ventured into my grandmother's rose garden. My grandmother often lamented the day she scolded Guildy for his trespass as her rosy retreat steadily became a haven for those pesky burrowing varmints resultant from Guildy's absence.

Guildy's loyalty was unquestionable. If a family member was confronted with danger, our Daschund would throw himself into harm's way with fearless abandon and complete disregard for his well being. I recall an unfortunate incident which occurred at a local store. Guildy and I had trekked to a small market not far from our house. I had just tethered Guildy to a post outside of the market when a bread vendor pulled in front of the store, got out of his vehicle and sharply told me to keep my dog away. I agreed, went into the store, made my selections, and was waiting to pay the clerk when I saw this man kicking Guildy. I immediately ran to assist my dog only to be pushed aside by the angered peddler. Guildy sprang into action, breaking his leash and attacking our assailant with such ferocity the aggressor fled the scene on foot. Fortunately, several people had witnessed the entire event and later attested to the innocence of both Guildy and myself, while stating the bread driver as the true villain of the whole affair.

Guildy was both long, and short in appearance giving him a humorous appeal. Often he would clown with our other animals in an attempt to play with them and get attention.

I recall one instance where he was successful in getting a chicken to play with him. He rolled and cavorted with one of our hens who in turn appreciated his comical maneuvers and played with him for several hours one afternoon.

It was hilarious watching those two very different animals chasing and prodding one another around our yard and those comical antics still fill me with laughter.

Guildy was an exceptional pet. His intelligence, obedience, loyalty and humor remain unforgettable, and I miss him dearly.

Tammy was my grandmother's pet Scottish Terrier and the third dog in my life. She was a typical Scotty — ornery, fearless, watchful of strangers, and extremely loving to members of her family. My grandmother loved Tammy as her favorite and the two of them were inseparable. No favor was too great for my grandmother's Little Scotch Duchess, and she spoiled Tammy inexorably.

I loved Tammy for her obstinate attitude. It was her way or the highway with that Scotty and compromise was never to be. Treats, pleading, and threats, were all useless in attempting to get Tammy to do one's bidding. Tasks required of Tammy were only completed after she decided it was time to do so.

Still, Tammy came on call, did her business outside, and never strayed from her yard, which made her a pretty good dog in my book.

Tammy's fearlessness can be illustrated in a story I recall from a morning long since past. Just before daybreak my grandfather released Tammy for a routine patrol of our property. Our petite black beauty was faithfully conducting her rounds when she came upon one of the neighbor's dairy cows and the ruckus began. My grandfather, grandmother and I rushed from the breakfast table to see what was causing the commotion. Tammy had immediately begun to evict the cow from our premises by incessantly barking and nipping at the wailing bovine's heels. I was astounded by Tammy's quickness and agility as she skillfully directed the cow homeward without getting kicked. This feat further amazed me because I knew that Tammy had no training or experience around livestock as she was my grandmother's house dog.

After the cow's retreat, my grandmother ran to her favorite's assistance. She picked up Tammy and showered her courageous little dark bundle with kisses while my grandfather and I stood dumfounded by the spectacle we had just witnessed. My grandmother ceaselessly praised Tammy all that day while reprimanding my grandfather for being so careless with her Little Scotch Duchess.

Tammy was an excellent watchdog and would not tolerate strangers or non-familiar family members anywhere on our premises. I remember a long ago episode involving some distant relatives who came to visit us from Canada.

My grandaunt and granduncle were wonderful pet loving people and everyone greatly appreciated their company except for the Little Scotch Duchess. Tammy felt these people were strangers and not to be abided.

When the day of Aunt Bunty's and Uncle Winn's visit came, Tammy was ready. It was as if she knew in advance some foreign entities were invading her domicile.

Our guests pulled up to the front of the house and were preparing to exit their vehicle when Tammy sprang into action. She shot out the door, dashed across the front yard and would not let either Bunty or Winn through the front gate. She barked and attempted to nip both our devoted relations in a malicious attempt to keep them from entering our yard.

This situation was truly embarrassing and it took my grandmother several minutes to calm and control her Little Black Beauty. Tammy finally accepted Aunt Bunty and Uncle Winn later that day and all was well until the next distant relative or far-off friend decided to pay our family a visit.

Tammy was a loving and loyal pet. She was always available to people she recognized as family and friends. Time and again she would come running to me and my buddies with licks and a wagging tail. She was special to me and I loved her very much.

The next member of my boyhood menagerie was Oliver.

Oliver was the pet rat that I adopted on a cold winter afternoon from a family who lived down the road. The Jones' raised rats to feed to their pet hawk and had an unusually abundant number of unwanted babies when my friends and I came to visit.

Debbie, a classmate of mine and the Jones' eldest daughter, had set up a makeshift stand along the side of the road. Duane, Spenser and I noticed the improvised booth and were curious to its purpose as we approached the

Jones' residence. Upon our arrival, Debbie immediately asked if I wanted a free rat while she put one of her baby rodents on my shoulder.

Oliver and I were bonded from the start. He wriggled and crawled around my neck and nestled under the collar of my jacket. I couldn't resist and took my adopted rodent home.

My grandmother was not pleased with the new pet I brought to the doorstep and told me to keep it under control or else.

I agreed, immediately drew every penny I owned and was off to purchase a cage. As I peddled my bike, I suddenly realized I didn't know anything about the care and feeding of rats. I was in a quandary. I had accepted a pet rat, promised my grandmother to care for it yet didn't have a clue about what to do or how much this venture would cost.

When I arrived at the local pet shop, I hurried to the owner and promptly asked him what seemed ten thousand questions about rats. Luckily, our pet shop was owned by Mr. Jordan, a kind man, who was very familiar with rodents and especially rats. He directed me to the rack of books that served as the "how to" section of his store. There before me was a virtual library for rearing and keeping rats. Mr. Jordan also had a wonderful supply of stock for the care of small animals..

I counted the money in my pocket carefully and had enough to get everything Oliver needed. I purchased; one of Mr. Jordan's books on Rat rearing, a cage, a water bottle, a food dish, a bag of litter and some rodent food for my little friend.

Oliver was off to a great start. I learned all about the care of rats and found them not only to be very intelligent but also very clean animals if given the opportunity.

Gradually, everyone in our family grew to love Oliver. I routinely cleaned his cage, gave him fresh water, and fed him the highest quality food. I also played with him every day which is very important toward the socialization of rats.

Oliver was a wonderful pet. He was highly intelligent, extremely clean, never bit anybody, was fun to hold and always did his business in one location within his cage.

Oliver lived for four years, an exceptional long time for a rat. Our vet said the reason for his prolonged existence was due to the great care and love our entire family bestowed on him.

I will forever remember the loving relationship I had with Oliver. I learned to overcome my prejudice against rats by caring for that marvelous little rodent. I also learned rats can be loveable and caring pats if given clean quarters and a loving home.

Narcissus was our proud pet goose. He was grafted into our family in an uncanny manner when I won him as a prize at a carnival. The story of Narcissus's adoption began on a hot July Southern Oregon evening when my grandmother decided to take me and several of my friends to a newly arrived traveling amusement park. The initial thought of going to a carnival was exciting, and our emotions steadily increased as our destination's bright lights and whimsical rides neared. We couldn't wait to squander our weekly savings on the carnivals attractions.

Soon, we were on the midway and I was playing every game available. One of those amusements featured a pond with swimming fowl as prizes. All that was required was to place a wooden ring on a peg placed some five feet distant. It didn't take long for me to complete the required task subsequently winning my feathered prize much to my grandmother's chagrin.

We didn't name my prize bird right away as we didn't know if our newest pet was male, female or even if he was either a duck or a goose. We also had questions about where and how to house our little friend. The answers to these questions were soon answered when we returned home and my grandfather inspected our newest family member. Grampa told us our feathered friend was going to be a male goose and he would probably be safe if we housed him with the chickens.

Surprisingly, he fit in with our chickens and was adopted by one of our hens. Our rooster left him alone and it was comical to see him follow his adopted mother around the yard while attempting to scratch for food. Eventually, we furnished him with a wading pool and our little gosling was very happy.

We puzzled on a name for our newest family member. However, it wasn't long before we discovered our prize gosling had an attitude and was very prideful. We decided to name him Narcissus after the egotistical Greek hero.

It was the perfect moniker for that arrogant bird and I

still recollect Narcissus parading around our yard, head held high and vigorously honking at anybody invading his sphere of influence.

Smokey, was our old horse. He was an Appaloosa my grandfather rescued from slaughter many years earlier. Smokey was a gentle animal and every kid in the area enjoyed riding him and feeding him carrots or some other indulgence.

Smokey occupied the pasture behind our house with Romeo, our pet bull. Both animals got along, never quarreled, and often could be seen grazing together.

We dubbed our pasture the Back Forty, because the area of fenced grazing land encompassed forty acres. Smokey loved the Back Forty, and it made me happy to consistently witness him blissfully cavorting in his pasture.

The Back Forty was where Smokey and I played together. Weather permitting, after chores, I would go to our pasture and give Smokey treats in exchange for a ride. He loved apples and I usually had my pockets filled with his favorite confection. I rode him bareback and he loped around the field at a gentle speed. I never hurried or rushed Smokey, and we both enjoyed those saunters very much. After our ride, I would brush him down, give him his oats then lead him to water and the barn at night.

I still vividly recall seeing Smokey waiting for me at the gate of the Back Forty as I approached from school. He would see me and begin to neigh. The sight of him and the sound of his neighing were comforting and the unfailing symbols of the home I loved

and longed for after each day of school.

I sorely miss the sight and sounds of that affable horse to this day.

Romeo was our pet bull and the largest of my boyhood animal friends. Romeo came to us as an esteemed Angus calf my grandfather purchased at the county livestock auction.

Romeo was immediately considered a member of our family. Yet, Romeo was different, and when he matured, he earned his keep handsomely. Romeo was my grandfather's prize breeding bull and there wasn't any luxury considered too extravagant to keep that blue blood bovine contented. Romeo was pampered from the first day he arrived.

He was brushed, bathed, fed the finest corn and oats as well as penned in the cleanest and most well appointed barn one could imagine. These extravagant practices were to assure Romeo as having a generous growth pattern, enhanced health, and a virulent physiology. It worked. Romeo turned out to be the biggest, handsomest, most potent, sought after Angus bull in Southern Oregon and my grandfather was always willing to tell you so.

Romeo was a good natured calf and enjoyed his life at our house. He would play with Butch, chase the chickens, and even attempt to befriend Narcissus, who usually was too impressed with himself to be bothered.

Eventually, Romeo became too big to be allowed in the yard. One day he decided to dine on a few of my grandmother's flowers while trampling our victory garden into nothingness. My grandmother was furious and demanded that my grandfather keep his *Spoiled Brat* out of the yard and away from her flowers. No amount of politicking could save Romeo and he was placed in the Back Forty during the day then in the barn at night. This arrangement was the same schedule we had for Smokey and everyone, except my grandfather, knew everything was going to be fine.

The next morning my grandfather released his pampered calf into the Back Forty. Romeo immediately bonded with Smokey and the two of them were instant friends. Smokey looked after Romeo and that little Angus calf followed Smokey around the pasture, never letting the old Appaloosa out of his sight. In the evening, we would call Smokey to the barn and Romeo would doggedly follow his equine leader inside. When morning broke, we opened the barn and Smokey would gently lead Romeo to pasture where the two of them would graze together throughout the day.

Romeo had a personality and a sense of humor. He liked to be teased and people in our neighborhood could not believe how I could goad a full sized bull without getting killed. Our game began with me approaching Romeo who was fully cognizant of my whereabouts and intentions. He would swish his tail as the only indication of his knowledge of our pending diversion. When I got close enough, I would slap Romeo on the rump as hard as I could. He would rise and playfully chase me throughout the pasture. After I tired, he would stop and come to me and gently nudge me with his head and moo very softly. I would conclude our engagement by softly rubbing his face and telling him what a good bull he was.

It was curious to watch Smokey and Romeo interact while observing their roles change as the years passed. Romeo became very protective of that old horse, only permitting myself and my grandfather to come near Smokey. Conversely, Smokey, aging and no longer the leader of the two, came to rely on Romeo for protection.

Often Romeo would be called upon to earn his keep. These trysts usually took several days and it was odd to see Romeo paying special attention to Smokey before departing.

It seemed our bull continually had premonitions about his pending exits and was worried about his equine friend. Normalcy returned when Romeo came home. The two of them could be seen cavorting around the Back Forty, genuinely happy to be in each other's company once more.

I'll always remember Romeo, the games we played, his sense of humor, as well as the love, tenderness, and caring, he routinely displayed. Romeo's emotional qualities were a source of wonder to me when I considered he was a full grown bull and though dramatically dissimilar in size, remarkably similar in attitude to the other domesticated pets I owned.

Hannibal, our pet rooster, was the tyrant of our barnyard.

He was a large Rhode Island Red and had an attitude to match his crimson plumage. Hannibal would not tolerate any strangers occupying his quarters and forcefully repelled all invaders.

Hannibal's history with our family began on a spring day when my grandfather decided it would be a good idea for me to learn animal husbandry via raising chickens. It was to be my job to feed, water and care for those birds as well as collecting their eggs for consumption on a daily basis.

The next morning we were off to the Big Y to select our chicks. I still remember looking into the large enclosure where the newly hatched poultry were housed and watching those little bundle of feathers squirming and running all over themselves. My grandfather selected approximately twenty females and one very active male chick. I thought they were wonderful and couldn't wait to play with them.

Upon returning home, my grandfather placed the chicks in their temporary enclosure and began to build their permanent housing with my fumbling assistance.

The coop was completed that afternoon and the chicks were placed in their new home. The chicks adapted well to their new surroundings. I watched over them carefully to assure their well being. If the evenings were too cool, we would bring our flock of chicks into the house, carefully placing them in my grandmother's warm kitchen oven for the night. I was astonished by the amount of food those little birds ate as they quickly grew into chickens.

Our little male chick soon became a large rooster. First, his little comb came into view, and then his bright red feathers began to appear. Finally his leg horns and bad attitude emerged.

My grandfather decided the name Hannibal would be suitable for such a large, cantankerous bird and this appellation suited him perfectly.

Hannibal was an excellent guardian of his brood but horrible to associate with if you weren't a chicken.

He recognized he could easily intimidate a young boy of seven years of age. I was terrified of that big red rooster, dreading to venture in the barnyard for any purpose.

Hannibal calculatingly realized I performed my chores at the same time daily. Those chores began with feeding the various animals of our menagerie. I would first go to the feed bins behind the barn, secure the feed necessary, and then give our animals their food. Hannibal's devious routine was to wait in hiding by the feed bins then ambush me at the first opportunity. He would pounce on my back, pecking me on the head, while wing whipping me until I fled the barnyard.

These painful attacks persisted and were becoming a problem. I complained to my grandfather only to receive a belly laugh and the advice to grow up. My dilemma escalated with Hannibal's attacks becoming more frequent and his pursuits extending down the driveway and out on the dirt road leading from our house. Somebody had to do something about this out of control rooster.

Hannibal's day of retribution finaly arrived. He met his waterloo on a warm summer afternoon my grandmother had chosen for hanging her laundry. As she busied herself she was unexpectedly attacked by our belligerent rooster. Nobody was there to witness the attack but it must have been substantial as my grandmother's neck, legs and arms were bloodied and covered with pecking marks.

I came home from swimming late that same afternoon and saw Hannibal, legs trussed, and resting upside down on his wings in the back yard. I went into the house and saw my grandmother lying on the sofa, heavily bandaged.

She informed me of Hannibal's treachery, finishing her comments with, "It's me or that stupid rooster."

I tended to my chores and waited for my grandfather to arrive from work, never daring to go near our fettered fowl lying exhausted in the summer sun. My grandfather came home directly and eying Hannibal's predicament, wanted to know what had transpired. My Grandmother calmly explained and gave my grandfather her ultimatum. I was told to continue with my chores while my grandparents worked out a compromise.

I never learned of the particulars of those negations, but my grandfather must have used the diplomatic skill of Disraeli to dissuade my grandmother from utilizing her guillotine style solution on our barnyard oppressor.

At the end of the day, Hannibal was allowed to stay with the caveat of being confined to the area designated for the chickens. Immediately, an expanded and fenced chicken pen was constructed. There were no more feathered attacks and Hannibal was freed from the chopping block as all barnyard matters quickly returned to normal.

Hannibal remained as our safely housed barnyard

tyrant for many more years. He was an excellent guardian of our chickens, keeping our hennery in good order. Yet, I will never forget the terror that rooster could engender, nor the havoc that resulted from his devious assaults.

Sammy was the final pet associated with my childhood past. He was a friendly little dog and unfortunately came to our home as a very sick stray. His stay with us lasted less than a year but the love we shared remains everlasting.

Sammy appeared on our door step on a cold December night. He was sick, shivering, starving, and must have been exposed to the elements for some time. We took him in with the collective knowledge of the jeopardy concerning his longevity.

We began to care for this piteous little dog by feeding him a meal of cottage cheese, eggs, and cooked rice. This concoction was recommended to us by our vet as a fail-safe remedy for dogs suffering from a variety of ailments. The concoction was moderately successful and must have been warm in addition to soothing for our small vagabond. Next, I gave our diminutive friend a warm bath. He liked the temperate water and nudged next to my arms as I gently scrubbed the accumulated grime from his frail body. The miniature dogs immediate care concluded with me gently placing him in a warm bed next to our furnace. He slept through the night calmly and was glad to see everyone in the morning.

Later the next day I decided to call our pocket-sized friend Sammy. The name seemed to suit him and he responded well to his new title.

Sammy was a mutt and looked to be part Chihuahua. He was smart and could perform several elementary tricks. We continued with his special diet and hoped Sammy would develop into a normal dog.

As the months passed and spring evolved, Sammy's health worsened. He never fully recovered from the feeble physical condition he suffered under when he first came to our doorstep. Sammy developed a persistent cough along with periodic seizures. Our vet couldn't cure him and we finally decided to put him down after only nine months of his loving company.

The loss of Sammy devastated me. I still can't fathom how somebody could abandon such a loving animal. My memory of Sammy's woeful destiny serves as a continual, glowing beacon illuminating the dastardly condition of abused and neglected animals in need of loving rescue.

The pets I enjoyed as a boy varied greatly in size, weight, appearance, and attitude. Nevertheless, I still consider those treasured animals as being part of the long lost family I still hold dear. The delightful, scary, amusing, and sad experiences, I had with my pets aided greatly toward giving me an insightful view of life and a deep regard for animals. These golden pet memories remain vital as part of the prized recollections I have of the bygone, idyllic household I shared as a boy.

Chapter 4

Chips Should Not Fly When Halloween is Nigh

My story, a tale of foolish pre-adolescent youth, contains drama, comedy, and a lesson learned.

The key characters involved in this episode include me, along with Spencer and Duane Poole. Duane was the leader of our group and Spencer was the youngest member of our band.

We had experienced our summer fling and now had been suffering under the unbearable rigors of school for over a month. Halloween was barely two weeks away and the thoughts of costumes and tricks and treats occupied our minds endlessly.

Friday afternoon finally rolled along and we were free from our prison of erudition. With only a couple of hours of daylight left in the day we had to find a form of recreation quickly. As we strolled down our dusty road toward home, I had a Hyperion moment of brilliance — my grandfather's cow pasture. With Romeo, our breeding bull, gone on an errand of husbandry, my horse corralled and the field full of fresh manure, it was the perfect venue for what I thought was just the thing to ease our juvenile tensions — a cow chip fight.

I immediately brought my idea foreword to the group and soon we were all flinging those disgusting patties at one another.

Unfortunately, the youngest member of our crew became our first and only casualty. I had taken dead aim at Spencer's left ear when he was momentarily distracted then adroitly placed a soggy clump of the foul material where intended. I still recall the concussing splat as the manure greeted the side of my friend's skull that ultimately sent him to the ground.

We concluded our amusement after approximately one hour of mayhem and decided it was time to go home and face our mothers. Spencer loved every minute of playing with the older kids and aside from shaking his head continuously, appeared to be fine.

Saturday began with chores. We each wanted to earn our allowance and we attended to our duties accordingly. Later that afternoon, our entire group got together and learned Spencer was really sick with an infection.

His ear had ballooned to twice normal size and was tomato red. Mr. and Mrs. Poole had rushed him to our distant county hospital where he was under medical treatment, soon to be fully recovered.

44

The days passed slowly in agonizing anticipation of the pending autumnal celebrations. My comrades and I had been saving our allowances for a month and Halloween was barely two days away when my friends and I decided to head for the Big Y to spend our accumulated wealth on costumes.

The Big Y was a huge emporium that housed within its confines a full service supermarket, a pharmacy, a department store, a nursery, a feed and seed store in addition to an auction yard. This was the perfect place to look for Halloween costumes.

After we arrived, we quickly made our selections and compared them with each other. It only took a moment to discover Duane's odd choice, a single exaggerated red ear of the type clowns wear in the circus. Duane donned the ear stating, "Trick or treat, I'm Spencer." Immediately, we were all convulsing in laughter with the exception of Spencer who was wailing and complaining of poor group dynamics as well as maltreatment.

After purchasing our treasures, we headed home with the Poole residence being our first stop. The distance covered was roughly three miles and the time it took to go from point to point was ample for Duane to taunt Spencer to the snapping point.

Upon arrival at the Poole residence we discovered Mr. Poole working feverishly in an attempt to replace the engine of his logging truck. Our approach must have been loud and maddening to my friends father as we marched the Poole's long driveway bragging of pending Halloween

exploits, Duane leading the way, ear clad and teasing his younger brother.

Suddenly, Mr. Poole emerged from his work and yelled at Duane, "Who the H _ _ _ are you supposed to be?"

Duane replied, "I'm going as Spencer for trick or treat."

Whereupon Mr. Poole responded, "No, you're not! You're grounded!"

The reaction to this announcement was immediate and threefold. Duane began to wail, Spencer began to laugh exuberantly, and the rest of us scattered like quail.

The following day arrived. It was Sunday, and Halloween was upon us. After dinner, we met at my house to ready ourselves. We were devising strategies for gaining the most candy in the least amount of time when our eyes were greeted with the sight of Duane and Spencer approaching. My friends and I immediately welcomed our two buddies. We were curious as to what had transpired in the Poole household over the past twenty-four hours. Duane explained he had decided to re-adorn himself as a pirate for trick or treat and Mr. Poole had correspondingly relented on Duane's punishment.

Our troop went on to enjoy a tremendous evening on that Halloween of my youth. Our strategy for obtaining the maximum amount of candy worked well, Duane and Spencer didn't squabble and everyone had a great time. Yet, the most valuable aspect of our long past sojourn on the eve of All Saints Day was the lesson that chips should not fly when Halloween is nigh.

Chapter 5

My First Fishing Trip

I still recall my first fishing excursion to the Cascade Mountains of southwestern Oregon. I was a boy of about seven years of age and my grandfather decided that Diamond Lake was the spot to introduce me to the sport of angling.

Diamond Lake is located within the Umpqua National Forest, approximately five miles north of Crater Lake. It's location, though remote, is easily accessible via highway, making it an ideal getaway. The lake sits at an elevation of 5,183 feet above sea level, has a nine-mile shoreline, and an average depth of 24 feet. Diamond Lake was formed by one of Mount Thielsen's primeval volcanic explosions. The lake filled with water from the melting glaciers of the last Ice Age. The lake was discovered by John Diamond in 1852 and has been a destination for anglers since the early part of the twentieth century.

The setting for my first fishing trip was beautiful, a crystal blue high mountain fishery nestled in an emerald green forest, with majestic Mount Nielsen crowning our view. Mother Nature cooperated — it was summertime, warm and not a cloud in the sky. I was amazed by the tame and docile wildlife. Both the deer and chipmunks would eagerly come to our cabin door and my grampa showed me how to hand feed our new wild animal friends potato chips and peanuts. Our quarters were rustic but well appointed and we had free access to a small boat.

We arrived at approximately 5:00 pm with high hopes and eager attitudes. My grampa rigged my equipment quickly and I caught the first fish of my life before dark.

This feat, though wondrous to me, was comical to my grampa and the other fishermen on the dock. I was excited and didn't have any idea of what I was doing. The only reason for my success was beginners luck. The fish was a Blue Gill and I still recollect the brilliant orange, green, and blue coloration of that handsome specimen. After breakfast, we gathered our gear and loaded the boat, then launched for our ultimate destination on the lake. I listened intently as my Grandfather took great care and time instructing me how to troll for trout while we chugged along in that old skiff.

Fishing with grampa was wonderful. His patience, understanding, sense of humor and expert knowledge endeared me to fishing as a lifetime pursuit.

Time and again I recall making mistakes, yet my grandfather never lost his temper. Instead, he offered a joke while correcting my error with a loving smile. As time passed, I became profoundly impressed by my grandfather's fishing skill. I felt fortunate for the opportunity to learn his angling secrets as they were lovingly passed down to me. It was almost dark when we headed back to the cabin with two limits of fish, my contribution being one trout I actually hooked, played and landed myself.

After dinner we joined the other fishermen around the campfire. A primal sense of camaraderie seemed to affect everyone as they shared their tales of accomplishment and glory. The stars, the flaming embers, the hooting of a distant owl and the collective feeling of happiness among all who attended still evoke deep feelings of contentment within me.

Ultimately, the various experiences associated with my first fishing trip continually call to mind pleasures of wondrous substance. The pastoral splendor, the tame wildlife and the pristine atmosphere astonished me. I can still recall the feeling of victory I experienced after catching my first fish and the tremendous sense of accomplishment I felt as I saw my grandfather beam with pride when I presented him with my first catch. I remember the patiently applied fishing knowledge I gained from my grampa's experience — our loving bond growing as we experienced the adventures of that beautiful trip, the wonderful campfire gathering and the primordial aura of friendship it fostered. Each of these experiences is unforgettable and fundamental to my appreciation of self, family, the wilderness, and especially fishing.

Chapter 6

Shootout at the Gravel Pits

Our boyhood adventures took many forms including bike trips, fishing excursions, hunting expeditions and rowdy jamborees — all fun and usually safe. Yet, I recall one foolish adventure quite different from the others, the shootout at the gravel pits.

The setting for my story was the gravel pits located on a local waterway approximately six miles from my house.

Our group had explored that region of the Rogue River a number of times. We would peddle our bikes doggedly to our watery retreat with each successive reconnoiter supplying more information and adventure.

One day, early in the summer, we discovered an abandoned gravel quarry. This facility was neither fenced nor posted and well suited to the attentions of a group of young, mischievous boys. At long last, we agreed an old rock quarry on the Rogue River was the ideal location for our latest caper, a B. B. gunfight.

We assembled the next day after chores to establish rules and picked sides for the coming battle. Rule number one was not to shoot above the waist of the opponent. Rule number two required all participants to wear at least two pair of pants thereby avoiding injury to body parts within the target area. Rule number three permitted surrender if a particular side was totally defeated. Rule four required both sides to re-select different members following a shootout in an attempt to add fairness to the bedlam. Once these preliminaries were attended to we picked sides, readied our weapons, mounted our bikes and were off to do battle.

As we journeyed to the gravel pits, everyone felt confident the pending mêlée would be conducted safely and sanely. Everyone was naively under the impression that the rules would be strictly obeyed without deviation or cheating.

In actuality, rules were broken, safety deviated from and cheating rampant from the onset of hostilities.

Upon arrival, we immediately separated into our two pre-selected sides. Each group comprised five boys who in turn strove to gain the high ground while taking shots at their respective opponents. The sting of the B B's became immediately apparent in spite of the layered clothing and wariness soon overcame valor.

Our imagined and valiant battle had quickly devolved into a series of ambushes and sniper missions. B. B.'s were flying everywhere and everyone was ducking for cover. I recall one confrontation where Harry routed Jimmy from his position behind some boulders. Jimmy quickly realized he was no match for his older brother and dropped his weapon then fled the field as fast as he could.

Harry kept firing and shouted, "Dance!" while his hapless younger sibling yelped, hopped and squirmed with each B. B. strike. Every exposed part of Jimmy's body soon became covered in stinging welts and the youngest member of our party was desperate to extricate himself from his painful circumstance.

It wasn't long before Jimmy began to wail with threats of tattling to their father. Harry kept firing on his brother until his supply of ammunition was exhausted. He then lowered his rifle considered the ramifications of his younger brother's threat and the skirmish between the two siblings ended.

Meanwhile, Duane and I had stationed ourselves atop a sizable pile of gravel where we commanded a view of the general area. Immediately, we saw Seth and Reuben attempting a similar maneuver as they scaled an old shack near the river's edge. The distance between our positions was roughly fifty feet, with their position considerably lower in elevation from ours.

Seth and Reuben were well within the range of our Daisy Red Ryders, and we began firing on the two brigands, shooting them off their positions quickly. We were elated with our brief victory and didn't realize how dire our predicament had become.

Suddenly, the tables turned — our lofty gravel refuge had become a shooting gallery with Duane and I assuming the role of clay pigeons. Seth and Reuben had retreated into a nearby brush- covered culvert free from danger, they began to sharp shoot the two of us.

In the meantime, Spencer and Heath had crawled behind a mound of discarded cement drain-pipes and were firing on Duane and I with equal accuracy from a position 180 degrees opposed to our first antagonists. We were pinned down in a crossfire atop our pile of gravel. B B's were hitting us everywhere each with the nip of a Bumble Bee sting. Within seconds, we dropped our guns and began to cry surrender.

The final skirmish of the day occurred across the abandoned loading yard of the quarry with the two most contradictory members of our group, slim, even tempered, Adam versus obese, ill-tempered Matt. This match-up reminded everybody of Laurel and Hardy and didn't disappoint in its comedic content.

Adam and Matt were in a standoff. Both combatants were well barricaded in opposing positions and shooting continually with neither in danger of being flushed into the open. Several minutes elapsed when Matt screamed abruptly and emerged from his lair, cussing and clutching his finger.

By some dazzling stroke of luck, Adam had struck Matt on the trigger finger.

Our assembly was held laughing while we watched Matt go into one of his notorious rages. This tantrum was a

dandy; it had all the aspects our group had come to expect when Matt went into orbit. He threw his gun, cussed each of us out, screamed at the top of his lungs and stomped on his bicycle.

Finally, Matt's anger subsided, he apologized to everyone and things returned to normal.

After resting and tending to our wounds, we decided to head for home. Our pace was slow due to a casualty of Matt's ire. His bike's front wheel was bent and wobbling as a result of his outburst and he could only maintain half speed. We didn't want to leave him behind, so we hung along with him all the way home. We chided one another as we peddled while our welts and fatigue reminded us there were no victors in this conflict.

Upon reaching home, we immediately went to our respective medicine cabinets and tended our wounds. After several hours of misery we met and decided B.B. gun fights were too dangerous. This lesson was well learned and we never engaged in that kind of activity again.

Chapter 7

Memories of Marvelous Crater Lake

Crater Lake is a wonderful National Park. The history of the reserve's volcano, Mount Mazama, continues to fill my mind with wonder. The beauty of the lake's crystal blue waters still enchants me as I remain in awe of the park's rustic alpine magnificence.

As a child I was delighted by the wildlife of Crater Lake and the eagerness of the animals to tamely approach me for treats and petting. I will forever recall the remote splendor of Crater Lake National Park and how it's alluring beauty filled me with the urge to experience mother-nature first hand. Its location was serene and I continually begged my grandmother to take me on trips to that remote parkland.

Crater Lake was a destination my Grandmother favored to illustrate the geologic wonders of the natural world. Gramma and I often made the two hour car ride along with those friends whose parents had approved the trip.

These were fun and exciting excursions and everybody couldn't wait to experience the natural marvels of that far away park land.

Our Crater Lake trips usually began at sun up as my grandmother lovingly packed our station wagon with a huge picnic lunch for all who could attend. Next, she counted heads, making sure everyone had a jacket, and then we were off.

I fondly recall our station wagon winding up the ribbon of highway as we made our way through the cool and shady forest to our destination. Suddenly there it was, Crater Lake, rising from the remote wilderness like a majestic jewel in the mid morning sunlight. The scent of cedar, pine and spruce, enveloped our car and immediately familiarized me with the presence of the surrounding forest.

We usually got to the park by 9:00 A.M. and stayed until almost dark. Our first stop was always the gift shop. I vividly remember seeing the painting of Mount Mazama mounted on a nearby wall. One of the park rangers was usually close at hand explaining the dramatic history of Crater Lake. I was amazed by that story, no matter how many times I heard it. Mount Mazama's once colossal size and volatile destruction continually filled my mind with the unlimited dimension of God's power.

We always were eager to explore the alpine splendor of the park after concluding our visit to the gift shop. I continually was enamored by the trees lining the perimeter of Crater Lake's rocky bowl, softening its harsh grey edges with emerald green boughs. I enjoyed the cool

shade provided by the lofty timber as it protected us from the blare of the summer sun. The crisp mountain atmosphere refreshed me and I was thankful to the forest for scrubbing the air clean of the impurities of civilization. I remember being astonished by Wizard Island, as it emerged from the azure blue water and forming itself on a lake created inside the crater of an extinct volcano. I especially appreciated the simple log cabin style architecture of the park's structures, which gave the area an aura of limited human interference. The extraordinary sights I remember of Crater Lake reflected the park's uncommon blend of geology, flora and fauna. I still have golden memories of that untouched topography and the beautiful wonders of Mother Nature that remained central and inspiring within Crater Lake National Park.

The crystal blue waters of Crater Lake captivated me. Sometimes we would take rides on the boat that ferried visitors around the lake and circled Wizard Island. Wizard Island was the top of the former Mount Mazama and remained as a tapered mass rising from the bottom of Crater Lake's waters. It stood as a mystic sentinel begging to be explored and captivating the imaginations of young boys such as my friends and myself.

I especially loved those crossings as our boat slid over the smooth cerulean blue water of that beautiful lake. I recollect the Ranger informing us as to Crater Lake being the deepest lake in the United States. This fact inspired me to envision horrifying deep water monsters lurking beneath and eyeing our unwary vessel as it charted its course.

As a young boy, I was always somewhat disappointed in our shipboard excursions to Wizard Island. I bemoaned never being attacked in like manner to Captain Nemo as he faced the giant squid.

Ultimately, our voyages to Wizard Island were always blissful and concluded without incident. Those pleasurable boat trips on that majestic body of water were always a favorite segment of our trips to Crater Lake National Park. The wildlife of Crater Lake was delightful. Animals were everywhere and we enjoyed feeding them very much.

The Chipmunks appeared as park ambassadors to my grandmother's picnic luncheons and unceremoniously snatched our handouts. The Stellar Jays, along with the Ravens soon joined our meal and were always available to vocalize their need for sustenance. The deer were usually more standoffish but could be enticed to attend our midday repast with an offering of potato chips. Other wildlife included; raccoons, possums and an occasional bear, however these last three species were never to be considered friendly and best viewed from a distance. The wildlife of Crater Lake was amusing as well as educational. I will always cherish the memories of the enchanting picnics we enjoyed with the creatures of God's genesis.

The trips we took to Crater Lake National Park were some of the most fantastic experiences of my life. I still vividly recall the rustic beauty of that parkland and my feeling of awe when I witnessed its wonders for the first time.

Our excursions to Crater Lake National Park were packed with fun and adventure.

Those outings instilled within me the desire to experience nature's splendor throughout my lifetime.

The beauty and wonder associated with those jaunts remain as the essence of my golden boyhood memories growing up in Southern Oregon.

Chapter 8

Y.M.C.A. Camp

Y.M.C.A. Camp was another golden experience I recall while growing up in southern Oregon. Y-Camp was expensive, yet always fun, and worthwhile. My friends and I looked forward to the fishing, boating, games, and hiking included in the camp program.

Our camp was male only, and located on the shores of its namesake, Diamond Lake. This beautiful body of water is located just north of Crater Lake in the majestic Cascade Mountain range. Diamond Y Camp was the ideal setting for boys to fish, play and learn about the wonders of nature. Our camp ran for two fun-filled weeks and usually began sometime in early July. The late start allowed the camp's ambient temperature to warm sufficiently to get the bugs working for great trout fishing.

The wonderful experiences I had on that majestic body of water remain unforgettable.

I'll always cherish the time I spent at Diamond Lake Y.M.C.A. Camp. Our thoughts of summer camp usually began in April, when the camp director came to our school with brochures. The promotional material outlined the camp well and included an explanation of costs. The fees for summer camp were high and everyone offset those costs by selling mints at fifty cents per box.

It must have been comical to our parents as they watched their offspring, melting boxes of mints in hand, repeatedly approach the same houses in the hope of making a sale. Incredibly, by late June, Seth, Duane, Spencer, Adam, and myself usually managed to have made enough money to pay our way to camp.

After two months of pedaling mints, we were running wild with anticipation; we couldn't wait for our biggest summer adventure to begin.

The fishing experience at Y.M.C.A. Camp was very special to me. My grandfather taught me to fish on Diamond Lake and I prized that body of water for the fond memories it engendered. The lake remained unchanged year after year, beautiful, remote and perpetually teeming with large, anxious trout. The vast numbers of eager fish made it easy for boys to catch a limit by simply casting spoons, or bobbing with night crawlers from the bank.

I recall a fishing experience I had at Y.Camp that included my friend, Seth, lots of fish and a lesson in fly fishing.

Early one evening after dinner Seth and I were discussing the best method to fish our camp's lake.

Seth promised to teach me the art of fly fishing and after I borrowed the proper equipment we were raring to go.

We decided to hike to the northern end of the fishery the next morning then work the main channel of the lakes inlet with dry flies. The hike was easy, and time passed quickly as we enjoyed viewing the wildlife along the way.

We arrived at the inlet before dawn, eager to catch tons of huge trout. Seth showed me how to rig my rod and cast a fly. I rigorously began working the water with a Royal Coachmen. Immediately, we each had a pan sized rainbow hooked and my friend showed me how to play my fish on a fly rod, I was very careful, bringing that trout in and I listened to Seth every inch of the way. I landed my first fly fished trout gently and was very proud of my new found angling expertise.

We kept rigging dry flies and casting them into the main channel of the inlet throughout the day. By noon, we had caught and released several nice rainbows. They were great fighters and I marveled at their bold coloration. We decided to keep fishing until dusk, never varying from our modus operandi of casting dry flies into the main channel of the lake's inlet and releasing the vast majority of our captured quarry back to the lakes watery realm.

At dusk, we decided to quit fishing and return to camp. Both Seth and I were glad to see the campfire and wanted to share our wonderful experience with everyone. Tom, our cabin counselor, was the first person to see us approach and asked how our angling excursion had turned out. We must have buried him with our exuberance. I couldn't shut up about my first fly fishing encounter.

Tom listened patiently and ultimately suggested we cook our fish over the campfire. Our trout tasted wonderful, cooked over an open fire with the stars twinkling above and my friends surrounding me. After dinner, we went straight to our cabin and were quickly off to the land of nod. I will forever treasure my first experience fly fishing on beautiful Diamond Lake.

Boating at Y. Camp was fun and provided new experiences to me and the other landlocked members of my group. Access to the camp boats was not given freely, however, and were to be earned. Basically, there were two camp requirements that had to be met before permission to check out a skiff was granted. First, all boating privileges were earmarked for older kids, who were at least twelve years of age. Second, a camper had to prove he could swim the required distance of a quarter mile before he could take a boat on the lake.

Boating placed me in a new dimension of travel to further explore that wonderful fishery. I remember one nautical adventure I had with Duane, Spencer and Adam which was fun, arduous, silly, amusing, and at the end of the day, curiously rewarding. Fortunately, all the members of our group qualified for the issuance of a boat except under aged Spencer, who became the first mate on Duane's boat.

Our adventure began early one morning when Duane and I announced to the camp populace the idea of rowing across the lake and back. This feat had never been attempted before, and we felt our three mile voyage was similar to that of Columbus, deserving like merit. Alas, this viewpoint was not shared by camp staff, much less by the other campers, who thought our proposal was a silly waste of time. Shocked by the negative reaction to our proposal, we decided to press on with our nautical mission into the unknown.

The next step of our journey concerned logistics.

We steadfastly marched to the dock and reserved two boats.

Actually, these boats were small rowing craft designed for fishing and not for grand scale exploration. Yet, we were willing to overlook this issue as a minor diversion from our glorious goal. After filling out the boat reservation forms, we loaded our lunches then set out on our crossing, certain our quest would be an easy and quick triumph.

It was a beautiful morning, no wind, and the lake was as smooth as a table top. We plotted our ship's course in an easterly direction and were rowing with jovial boldness when a light breeze came up. The first zephyr refreshed, cooling us as we labored forward.

Our fortunes soon changed when the breeze turned into a twenty mile an hour wind blowing in our faces. The uncomfortable gale did not dissuade us and we doggedly continued to toil through the lake's chop. As I rowed, I recalled the galley scenes from the movie Ben Hur. I empathized with the hero stoically rowing his warship exhausted and suffering. Thankfully, the wind didn't gather any more speed and we slowly continued our journey across the lake. We stopped at midday to rest on the eastern lake shore, and decided to eat our lunch in the shade of the lofty pines that densely populated the area. Suddenly, we were unceremoniously greeted by several of our fellow campers. They rebuked us for undertaking such a silly venture, while touting the fact of effortlessly beating our time across the lake, on foot, following the shoreline. We were too tired to snub our antagonists and quietly boarded our skiffs for the last leg of our journey.

The wind had stopped and we made it back to camp before dinner. We were bushed. Spencer and Adam lay down on the dock to rest while Duane and I checked in the boats. The four of us returned to the main lodge and found ourselves the subjects of everyone's amusement. Jokes, and pantomime impressions of our journey flourished. We countered these camp insults with the dignity of accomplishment, and challenged all campers to match our feat. Everybody eventually agreed our mission, though foolish, was something no other camper had ever done.

We were awarded for our efforts by the presentation of a broken old oar. This useless piece of equipment was to be signed by every member of our expedition, and placed on the wall of the dining hall, just above the garbage cans. The irony of our foray into the unknown was now complete.

The games we played at camp were a lot of fun and everybody got involved. Capture the Flag, Grease the Watermelon and Splatter Ball were a few examples of the diversions we enjoyed in the afternoon before dinner. These amusements were closely regulated by the counselors

to assure nobody got injured, and sides were always adjusted for fairness after a contest. Team captains were appointed by the camp staff and teams were selected by the pick and choose principle.

Capture the Flag is a martial oriented game of conquest between two opposing teams. Each team's ultimate goal is to capture the flag located on their opponent's fort. The secondary goal of tagging, capturing and jailing every member of an enemy team is pursued in accordance with a team's primary goal.

Following the appointment of captains, and team selection, boundaries and territories for each side were agreed upon. The placement of forts and team flags within each team's respective territories was then recognized. Finally, jails were designated within the boundaries selected for each team.

The fun associated with this game began with the unlimited strategies and scenarios that developed pursuant to each team's goals. The strategic value of a team's plan was measured in its effectiveness of capturing the opponent's flag as losses mounted and fatigue set in. The winning team was declared when an opponent's flag was captured.

Duane and I were very good at the game of Capture the Flag. We always worked to enlist the fastest and most agile campers to be members for our team. Our strategies and diversions were well timed and we usually captured our opponent's flag in a short period of time.

Unfortunately, our reign of terror in the game of Capture the Flag was not long lived, due to the vigilant eye of camp staff. Duane and I were rarely allowed to be members of the same team and we typically opposed one another on those imaginary fields of battle. However, I recollect those games of Capture the Flag fondly, never to be forgotten.

Grease the Watermelon was an aquatic styled game we enjoyed. This game was especially popular on those hot July afternoons. The cool water soothed and the prized watermelon refreshed every camper who participated in those sodden competitions.

Teams and captains were designated for Grease the Watermelon in the same way as Capture the Flag and counselors were omnipresent to guarantee fairness and safety.

The beauty of Grease the Watermelon existed in the game's simplicity and satisfaction. Each team positioned themselves waist deep in the lakes cool waters and struggled to obtain sole possession of a greased watermelon bobbing nearby. The grease applied to the skin of the Watermelon was Vaseline and harmless for consumption as well as to the ecology of Diamond Lake.

Victory was declared when one team was able to bring their slippery reward to the lake shore and present it to the counselors for all to consume.

I yet recall the feeling of those slick watermelons slipping from my grasp as we dunked and splashed one another in the invigorating lake water during those sweltering summer afternoons. I can still taste the marvelous flavor of those summer gourds and hear laughter envelop me after those soggy contests.

These are but a few of the golden memories I have playing Grease the Watermelon at Y.M.C.A. Camp.

Splatter Ball was my favorite camp game. I enjoyed the mayhem the game created when two teams lined up and tried to eliminate one another by tagging opposing team members with volleyballs.

Teams and captains for Splatter Ball were established with the same protocol of the other camp games. As always, these diversions were well supervised by a vigilant staff who assured the pursuit of fair play and safety. I cannot recall anybody ever getting hurt playing this unruly pastime.

The popularity of Splatter Ball was due to the antagonistic and fast moving action this activity contained. The time for set up was minimal, rules were simple and equipment needed was minor. A soft grassy area was first selected. This spot had to be large enough to accommodate two teams of approximately twenty-five boys. The ground had to be soft, rock free, absent of gopher holes and reasonably level. Once a field of play was selected, the boundaries for the game were chalked off.

There were only four rules pertaining to our camp's version of Splatter Ball. These rules were always carefully reviewed by camp staff before play to assure complete understanding and staff control. First, everyone had to play the whistle, to assure game management. Second, head shots were strictly forbidden in the cause of safety. Third, a player had to leave the field immediately after being tagged, to guarantee game progression.

Finally, an equal number of volleyballs were given to each team to assure fairness. These regulations assured safety while allowing a large and rowdy group of pre-adolescent boys to exhaust themselves quickly and safely.

Play began with a blast from a counselor's whistle and the carnage began.

Contests rarely lasted longer than five minutes, and it was great fun running, jumping, and dodging balls. Victory was declared after one team eliminated all the members from the other team by tagging them with volleyballs. New captains were then appointed by the counselors, teams were selected and a new contest of Splatter Ball was begun.

This continuum of activity remained in place until every camp member was exhausted and the peaceful ambiance of our campground was restored.

Hiking was another camp activity appreciated by every camping member. The various trails provided our young trekkers with a varied selection of opportunities for viewing the alpine scenery and photographing wildlife. Even so, there was one hiking expedition every camper wanted to be involved with — climbing Mount Thielsen.

Mount Thielsen is located approximately three and one half miles to the east of Diamond Lake. Thielsen's peak rises imposingly above the lake's surface as a rocky spire. That lofty pinnacle was always in view and challenged our young egos.

The mountain has a similar history to Mount Mazama and was once an active volcano that last erupted over two hundred and fifty thousand years ago. Mount Thielsen remains as the tallest of the Oregon Matterhorn's with a peak elevation of nine thousand one hundred and eighty three feet. The mountain was named after Hans Thielsen, a railroad engineer who pioneered the Oregon/California Railway.

Our trek to the top of Mount Thielsen began immediately following breakfast and lasted through the day to suppertime.

Camp staff members were continually available as guides and made sure we all had a hearty lunch. Exploring Mount Thielsen was both pleasant and interesting, with wildlife and the scenic splendor of the cascade forest to enchant. The climb was interesting and not especially grueling with the exception of the last eighty feet to the top of the peak. I still recollect the majestic view I had from Thielsens summit. Several landmarks were clearly visible as I gazed at the geologic splendor of my camps surroundings.

Our hike began with a bus ride from camp headquarters to the mountain trail head. Once at the trail head, we journeyed through the forest and up the mountain. At first, the grade was minimal and allowed everybody to get acclimated to the hike while enjoying the sights of the forest. I still recollect the dramatic change of scenery as we hiked on through the tree line.

The treeless landscape resembled the surface of the moon and I marveled at the dichotomy of Thielsen's vista as I looked back on the lush vegetation below.

The pumice we encountered above the tree line was interesting. I never imagined the experience of trudging through such a vast amount of material I knew as the main ingredient to a familiar brand of soap. I was amazed when one of our counselors illustrated the buoyant qualities of pumice when he floated a piece of this rock in a cup of water.

Shale was another interesting rock formation we came upon as we hiked above the trees to Thielsen's summit. This dark rock lay thick on the trail, and made it difficult to proceed due to the loss of traction, as it gave way under everyone's footsteps.

At last, our goal was within reach — we made it to the base of the mountain's spire just before noon and were anxious to finish our climb. Mount Thielsen's pinnacle, a nearly 25 meter pointed mass of volcanic rock must be approached with a degree of care and rock climbing acumen.

Fortunately, our guides were well versed in rock climbing and everyone was able to take turns reaching the top of Thielsen's peak and signing the included log book.

Hiking to the top of Mount Thielsen was one of my biggest boyhood achievements. I truly felt I had accomplished something as I gazed at the setting below. I was astonished by the beauty of the scenery as I viewed hundreds of miles in every direction. The visual spectacle from Thielsen's summit and the feeling of accomplishment I felt when I topped that mountain still linger within my memory as a significant boyhood accomplishment.

The experiences I had attending Y.M.C.A. Camp were wonderfully rewarding in several ways.

The encounters I had fishing, boating, playing games, and hiking, helped to shape my continued appreciation of the outdoors.

The mentoring, guidance, and opportunities provided by the camp staff were excellent and gave me a sound background in leadership. Finally, the Christian oriented camp program provided me with a fundamental appreciation of man's purpose and position within Mother Nature's cathedral. I will never forget my golden experiences at Diamond Lake Y.M.C.A. Camp.

Chapter 9

Bike Trips

Bike trips were a way of life for both my friends and I as we grew up in southern Oregon. The long distances between ports of call within our rural environment required some form of wheeled transportation be available. The hundreds of trips we took were often ten miles or more and covered the valleys, hills, and flats of our regional domain.

We treasured our old, two speed, balloon tire bikes due to the freedom they provided. We gave those bicycles a lot of attention as well as maintanance, and they never let us down providing the transportation for our boyhood adventures.

Hookey bobbing was a foolish technique my friends and I employed to assist our efforts on those long bike rides. We engaged this technique by peddling our bikes close behind logging trucks then grabbing hold of the trucks rear fender as it chugged in the direction we wanted to go.

This method, though dangerous, was effective, and we could cut our traveling time dramatically if we hooked enough rides.

Hookey bobbing infuriated the truck drivers and they unerringly complained to my grandfather whenever my friends and I attempted this stunt. My grampa would then inform the parents of those involved, and punishment was administered. The punishment I received for hookey bobbing was usually the impoundment of my bicycle for several weeks.

This chastisement was very effective, leaving me grounded with plenty of time to assist my grandma with chores such as hanging laundry.

The Applegate River was one of our most frequent destinations. We favored this area for the countless fishing and swimming opportunities it provided, and considered its long and winding access well worth the effort. The Applegate runs approximately fifty-one miles from its headwaters in the Siskiyou Mountains of northern California, to where it empties into the Rogue River six miles west of Grants Pass.

The distance from my house to the Applegate River Valley was a little over twenty miles and took several hours to cover one way. We fished the river before it was dammed and the valley was developed. I still recall with fondness those golden summer afternoons riding our bikes to that Eden in the hills.

I remember one trip Duane, Seth, and I took to one of our favorite fishing spots. It was summer and the beautiful pools of the Applegate were just the thing to cool us off. The morning of our departure began with excitement as we loaded our bikes with our fishing tackle, along with our lunches and looked forward to a great day of fishing.

Our destination was the Upper Applegate River above its confluence with the Little Applegate River. We started our trip early, hooked a few rides, and after a couple of hours reached our port of call. Deer, wild turkey, quail and other wildlife were everywhere within the lush environment of the river. The water was chilly and its magnificent aqua marine blue color invited.

The morning sun still lay hidden behind the hills, and the three of us sat on the bank eyeing over the rivers pools for fishing possibilities. Things looked good. We turned to Seth to plan our angling strategy, then began to fish. The worms we decided to use worked well and we caught our limit by 11 a.m. We cleaned our catch immediately, storing them in the river's nippy water for preservation.

The summer sun shone fully upon us as morning passed to afternoon. While we sweltered, Duane looked to Seth and I, then stated, "What are we waiting for."

Instantly, we followed Duane's lead and dove into the river without bothering to remove our clothes. The water felt wonderful as we splashed and dunked each other to cool off.

After refreshing ourselves thoroughly, we decided to head home. The ride back from the Applegate Valley was easy, down-hill most of the way, and I was showing my informed grandfather my catch before dark.

81

He quietly assessed my catch, and then impounded my bike for two weeks stating, " Hookey bobbing was a foolish way to catch a limit of fish."

How could he have found out about my highway transgression so quickly? I was dumbfounded and left to contemplate my error as I tended to extra chores around the house during my term of impoundment.

Mount Roxy Ann was another spot we chose as a destination for our bike trips. Roxy Ann is actually more of a hill than a mountain, but its steep grade was a huge attraction for downhill bike racing. Mount Roxy Ann is approximately thirty million years old and has an origin as a volcano. Roxy Ann lay just east of Medford and her peak was an easily visible landmark for most of the Rogue River Valley.

The trip to Mount Roxy Ann was considerably shorter than the trips we took to the Applegate Valley, requiring a correspondingly lesser amount of time and effort. The distance from my house to Prescott Park, near the peak of the mountain, was just over ten miles. The roadway was mostly level as well as paved, and with the exception of Roxy Ann Road, an easy ride.

I remember one trip I took with Adam, Harry, and Jimmy one Saturday in late spring. We had packed our lunches and binoculars quickly and left my house around noon. The ride was our first of the season, and our eager senses were bombarded with the color of flowers and the smell of green grass. We made Prescott Park by early afternoon and stopped for lunch. I enjoyed watching the eagles, falcons, hawks, quail, and turkeys while we ate, and I was glad we had made the trip.

After lunch we pressed on to the top of Roxy Ann. I'll forever recollect the view as I lovingly gazed down at my home valley. I could clearly see several points of interest around Medford. It was interesting to watch the toy sized planes of the far away airport take off and land as well as the distant, mite sized, cars traveling the black ribbons of ash fault en route to their assorted destinations.

After viewing the sights of the Rogue River Valley, our thoughts turned to our favorite part of the trip, the downhill race home. We began by racing our bicycles down the gravel road from the peak to Prescott Park. Our only casualty in this segment of the race was Jimmy, who failed to make the sharp turn just below the park, and skidded into the ditch along the shoulder. From the Prescott recreational area we continued our descent to the base of the mountain. Adam and I had become very skilled at coasting, braking, and pedaling our bikes, but Harry was the true cycling expert of Roxy Ann Road. We covered the four mile downhill trek quickly, leaving Jimmy far behind. Harry, easily won the race to the bottom of the hill, where Adam and I congratulated him accordingly.

We rested by the side of Hillcrest Road while we waited for Jimmy to arrive. Our bedraggled straggler finally appeared. We checked our bikes, then rode the rest of the way home leisurely satisfied with the idea of once again conquering that mighty mountain.

The Rogue River was our most frequent cycling destination because the seven miles of paved road leading to Touvelle State Park was level and easy to peddle a bike over.

My friends and I would often take the trip to the Rogue to swim, fish, or just have fun. However, the area around Touvelle Park held an irresistible mystery for me and my intrepid band of cyclists — long lost treasure.

The story of "The Lost Treasure of the Rogue River" began with my grandfather, who told my friends and I of slot machines, filled with money, that were supposedly dumped into the river, near Touvelle Park, after gambling in Oregon was abolished many years earlier. This malarkey pricked our pre-adolescent imaginations and our boyhood cupidity goaded us on while we dreamed of vast, undiscovered riches lying in the depths of the Rogue's waters, just a short Bike ride away.

Our group of would be treasure hunters began our escapade early one summer afternoon. We loaded our lunches, packed our swimming masks along with our swim fins, and were off to discover incalculable riches.

We made the river by one o'clock and agreed to search the entire afternoon. The plan was to separate into teams and reconnoiter the area above and below Touvelle Park. We separated into two squads of divers, each responsible for searching a side of the Rogue as far as possible by four o'clock. One team took the north side of the river and comprised Seth, Reuben, Jimmy, Adam and myself, while Duane, Spenser, Heath, Harry, and Mark made up the other team who explored the river's south side. After everyone was briefed and certain

of their assignments we stripped to our bathing suits, donned our diving gear, and immediately began searching the shallows of the watercourse for those anticipated riches. After only a few minutes we were reminded how inhospitable the Rogue could be. The river's cold water forced us from our quest and we spent most of our time warming ourselves on the sunlit banks of Touvelle Park. As we sunned ourselves, we began to evaluate our circumstances and discussed whether or not to continue. Soon, our unity of purpose began to crumble. Spencer and Jimmy had gotten chilled, and didn't want to continue. Seth was bored with the idea of our expedition and decided to fish the river instead. Adam began to question the truthfulness of my grandfather's story, while Duane and Harry had to leave in order to get their freezing little brothers home before they got sick. In the meantime, Mark had thrown his swimming mask into the trees after he got frustrated with its constant leaking and was cussing everyone out for his ordeal.

Now only three treasure hunters remained to glean the enormous lost riches of the Rogue. Heath, Reuben, and I pressed on with our mission by wading the chilly shallows of the waterway. It was getting late when we found some rocks containing, "gold". This unexpected discovery lifted our sagging spirits and we forgot about the mystery of the lost slot machines. Our boyhood optimism was sky high and we prodded each other onward with fantasies of avariciousness

We hurried to get all the precious rocks we could carry and scrambled from the water and up the bank to our bikes. The three of us mounted our mechanical steeds and headed for home with as much "gold" as we could fit into our pockets and satchels. We peddled the flats as fast as we could and I couldn't wait to show my grandfather our newly acquired riches. I stormed into the house shouting, "We're rich," and then dashed to show the old story teller my bounty as he sat in his easy chair.

My grampa immediately began to laugh as my gramma looked at me with a puzzled expression. I mistook both reactions, thinking my grandmother was confused by my outburst, and my grandfather was giddy with the thought of our sudden wealth.

Unfortunately, I was wrong on both counts. My grandfather wasn't laughing with me, he was laughing at me. My grandmother looked puzzled because she wondered how I could have gotten my clothes so filthy in such a short time.

After my grandfather finished laughing, he explained the gold I discovered was pyrite or fool's gold. He also explained this mineral was worthless and that I wasn't the first person to be fooled by the false majesty of pyrite's specter. I was deflated and immediately vowed to never search for lost gold again.

This vow was quickly broken after my grandfather lured Adam, Duane, Spencer and I to the back porch of our house one summer evening a few weeks later.

As twilight turned to darkness, my grampa sat us down and spun a new tale of lost riches. This was all the motivation we needed and the next day my friends and I were off chasing after another fantasy on our magnificent fat tire bikes. The bike trips we took throughout the Rogue River Valley were fantastic as well as unforgettable.

I'll forever recollect hookey bobbing and the beautiful trout we always caught on those trips up the Applegate River. I still recall the sights, the smells, and the wildlife—in addition to the breakneck races that were a part of those cycling trips to Mount Roxy Ann.

I also remember the fruitless treasure hunts we conducted in search of mysterious lost Rogue River gold. Each of those experiences was made possible by those sturdy, old, standard bicycles that gave us the freedom to experience the beauty and wonder of the bucolic environment that was so much a part of the golden years of my boyhood.

Chapter 10

Model Airplanes

Building and flying model aircraft was an activity several members of our group enjoyed. The field behind my house was my grampa's irrigated pasture land, and we utilized its wide open spaces for flying fields. That grazing land was ideal to our flight purposes for two reasons. First, the alfalfa was always moist providing a soft and fire safe ground surface in the event of crashes. Second, that pasture was fenced and when the field was vacant the fences kept unwanted interference from sheep, cattle, or Smokey and Romeo to a minimum.

Electronic remote control was not yet widely available for model aircraft and our kits were primitive by today's standards. Harry had the most experience flying model aircraft and was always available to help Jimmy, Adam, and I with the numerous problems we encountered constructing those complex models.

Harry was several years older than the rest of us and had built and flown many kits before we got our start in the hobby. He had acquired a variety of skills building and flying balsa wood model airplanes including rubber band powered aircraft and gas powered models in a variety of applications.

Under Harry's direction, the three of us began our model aviation experience with stick built balsa wood kits. These kits were relatively cheap and taught us the basic principles of flying. We began with rubber powered models, then moved on to free flying gas powered aircraft, and finally advanced to gas powered control line models.

The rubber powered aircraft we built was elemental and taught us how to frame, tissue, and fly model airplanes. With Harry's assistance, we learned the principles of wing loading and power to weight ratios, as well as correcting our planes from the uncontrollable characteristics of stalling, excessive pitching, excessive yawing, and rolling.

Our rubber powered planes flew without pilot input and as fledgling modelers we had to be sure factors such as center of gravity, rudder offset and lift had to be accounted for during the building phase of the models we were working on. Those kits had to be built light to accommodate the gliding phase of their flights after their elastic power ran out. Conversely, our rubber powered models had to be built strong enough to handle the rigors of hand launching and pilot-less landing.

Finally, those diminutive aircraft had to be built in a way to allow easy repair in the case of a crash.

Our elementary phase flying models were powered by a large rubber band placed within the fuselage of the airplane.

One end of the rubber band was attached to the propeller, and the other end was attached to a dowel placed in the aircraft's tail. The rubber band was then wound via turning the propeller until tight, to store elastic energy. Once the rubber band was wound sufficiently, the propeller was held stationary, then simultaneously released as the plane was thrown into the air.

The stored elastic energy of the coiled rubber band provided the power for flight as the model gained altitude. After the elastic energy was exhausted, the plane became a glider and with luck floated to the ground safely.

I recall the first rubber powered model I constructed. It was a replica of a Piper Cub and had a wingspan of fourteen inches. I was very careful constructing that kit; I wanted to impress Harry with my building skill as well as with my model's flight performance. The little yellow plane turned out great and I couldn't wait to show it to my mentor.

Harry was impressed, and wanted to go out immediately and fly my aircraft. It didn't stall, pitch, or yaw excessively, and gently rose to an elevation of 10 feet before gliding in for a soft landing. I was relieved and proud as Harry told me I had done a good job. I kept that little Piper Cub for several years and flew it many times.

While I was building my Piper Cub, Adam had been working on a kit of his own. It was a P-51 Mustang and he had done a superb job of construction. Adam was showing off his silver war bird to everyone one day when Harry appeared and asked to see Adam's model.

Harry looked the P-51 over carefully and complimented Adam for his craftsmanship.

We immediately took the Mustang out to the flying field for a test flight and it passed with flying colors. Harry and I congratulated Adam for his success and wondered what model airplane the smallest member of our group was going to build.

Unfortunately, Jimmy was not the craftsman we were. He often got impatient then rushed the construction of his model airplanes and consequently Jimmy's kits didn't always turn out well. Harry would scold Jimmy for his poor efforts then scornfully dismiss his younger brother. Jimmy took this to heart, and realized this was something he couldn't finagle his way through. He buckled down and worked hard with the hope to one day build a model airplane that could compare to his older brother's kits.

I recall the day Jimmy built his first successful model aircraft. His triumph came in the form of a rubber powered Nieuport. Jimmy had really taken his time to craft this kit and it showed. The framing was true, the tissue was applied correctly and the color scheme was exact. Jimmy's model was a well-crafted replica of the planes that flew in the Hat in the Ring Squadron during the First World War.

Early one summer morning, Jimmy brought his plane forward for his older brother to inspect. Harry liked what he saw, gave Jimmy a brotherly vote of respect, and we rushed to the pasture to see if the World War 1 model could fly as good as it looked. That little Nieuport was fantastic; it climbed into the air, without stalling, then floated like a Butterfly and gently landed in the cool alfalfa without incident. Harry was proud and Jimmy finally felt acknowledged by his elder sibling.

Adam and I begrudgingly congratulated Jimmy for his efforts then rushed home to count our money and plan for the next model aircraft we were going to construct.

The Nieuport's performance made both Adam and I feel a little jealous. Jimmy's plane flew as well as the aircraft we were flying and we obnoxiously refused to accept Jimmy or his skillfully constructed kit. Harry noticed our immaturity, and treated Jimmy, Adam, and I to sodas at the Big Y.

Harry suggested we should work together and learn from each other's errors as well as accomplishments to become better pilots and model builders. We listened to our mentor and decided he was right. At last we were "The Four Aces of Elliott Road."

After constructing and successfully flying several rubber powered kits, Jimmy, Adam, and I progressed to gas powered free flight models. These planes were much larger, possessing wingspans up to five feet or more, with engines ranging from the popular .049 to .35 and higher. The dimension of these gas powered model aircraft was far greater than the dimensions of our rubber powered models and required more time for construction and more shop space to accommodate the larger wings and fuselages. We also had to account for new components such as engines, fuel tanks, and flight timers.

Operationally, the transition from flying rubber band kits to flying free flight models was easy because both types of aircraft were assembled, launched and flown in a similar way. The gas powered free flyers were also constructed with their controls built into the aircraft structure to allow stable pilot-less flight. Here, as with the case of the rubber powered planes, undesirable characteristics such as stalling, excessive pitch, excessive yaw, and rolling were eliminated during the building phase of the kit.

Our gas powered free flight models had to be built strong enough to withstand their added size and weight as well as the rigors of being literally thrown into the air during launch.

Conversely, those free flyers had to be light enough to turn into gliders, ride the air and safely land after their fuel was depleted. This strength to weight dichotomy took each of us a little time to master before we were able to build and fly aerodynamically sound aircraft.

The first thing Jimmy, Adam, and I found to be new and different was the cost associated with gas powered free flight models. These kits were expensive in relation to the smaller rubber powered models we were familiar with.

Accessories such as the engines and fuel dramatically increased the cost of not only the construction, but the operation of those bigger kits. These factors forced us to quickly realize flying this type of aircraft required planning, as we could afford only one plane per year.

The kit I selected as my first engine powered free flight aircraft was a Fokker E 1. It had a wingspan of three feet, a fuselage length of 24 inches and was powered by a .049 cu. in. engine. I offset the cost of my newest plane by saving all the money I could and doing extra chores around the house. The expense connected with that kit made me extra careful, and I continually pestered Harry during every step of its construction. He was ceaselessly available to assist me with questions concerning breaking in my motor, framing, the application of dope, or a thousand other problems associated in building engine powered model aircraft.

I finally completed my fire engine red Fokker in just about three months. Harry inspected my work extra carefully, due to the enhanced danger of flammability from fuel and a hot engine. My latest creation passed its pre-flight flight test easily. The control surfaces were correctly aligned, the framing was straight and true, the engine was mounted properly, and the entire aircraft was fuel proofed.

Harry said I was ready and that he would help me take my plane to our flying field in the morning.

We arrived at the pasture early to take advantage of the calm air. Harry advised it would be best if he took over to allow me to watch him safely fuel and start my motor. All went well, no reverse starts and my little motor was humming like a bee.

Harry let that little engine run for a minute or two then killed it and inspected all the vital points of my model for problems.

Again, everything was o.k. and we were ready to fly.

Harry restarted my motor, and then launched my plane and she rose into the sky in concentric circles achieving an altitude of a couple of hundred feet. This flight path was pre–planned by building a fifteen degree offset into the rudder.

Harry had purposefully filled the tank half way to allow a shorter flight time, and my Fokker began to glide after only a couple of minutes of powered flight. She floated gracefully on the soft morning air of summer then landed gently in the tall alfalfa. I was happy with my achievement and I flew my E 1 often during that wonderful summer.

95

Adam had also selected an engine powered free flight airplane to build and fly. His aircraft was much larger than mine, having a wing span of over eight feet, a 48 inch long fuselage and a powerful .35 cu. in. motor. Adam's kit was called the Ramrod 500 and was not only bigger, but much more complex than my free flyer. Early on, it became apparent that Adam would need a lot of Harry's help if that big ship was going to be a success.

Adam went to Harry almost immediately and asked for assistance with his giant model. Harry agreed to help Adam and offered his spacious shop, recently converted from his dad's old garage, to use as a hangar. Things worked out fine and they began to build that huge ship in earnest.

The Ramrod 500 build progressed rapidly. Jimmy and I would make frequent visits to Harry's hangar and snoop to see how things were going. That ship was the biggest flying model we had seen and we were impressed. Adam had done a great job building the huge double dihedral wing, while Harry completed the fuselage, rudder, and elevator with his customary degree of excellence. Adam named his kit The Empress and painted her cub yellow to stand out against the sky. Harry completed the engine's break in and testing on Adam's thirty-five, then mounted that large power plant on the fuselage.

Adam installed the spring loaded fuel timer as well as the fuel tank and his colossal free flyer was complete.

The next morning Harry and Adam went to our pasture to fly The Empress, while Jimmy and I followed as onlookers.

The test run of the motor went without a problem. Adam gave his ship a final inspection, and everything was a go.

96

After starting the motor and setting the fuel timer, Harry handed "The Empress" to Adam for launch.

Adam gave his plane a mighty heave and she rose to the heavens easily in accord with the pre-designed offset of the rudder.

Harry had set the fuel timer to three minutes, preventing Adam's plane from flying beyond sight of the naked eye. However, nobody could have predicted the thermal that lifted and pushed Adam's ship as high and as far as it did.

Fortunately, Harry had brought a pair of binoculars and he spotted "The Empress" as she continued to climb the air in a heading toward White City, some nine miles away.

We quickly mounted our bikes, and followed Adam's plane as she flew in a northeasterly direction.

Thankfully, the updraft pushing that runaway model died down, and she slowly began to descend to the ground just a couple of miles from her take off point. She landed softly in an open field of star thistle and sustained only minor damage. Adam was relieved that he had not only found his free flyer, but also retrieved it in relatively good condition. Harry gave "The Empress" a thorough post flight inspection, then we mounted our bikes and headed for home with Adam's wayward masterpiece in tow. Harry helped Adam repair "The Empress," and she was able to make many more successful flights during that warm and wonderful summer.

Jimmy had also had been saving his money, and along with the funds he earned from extra chores, as well as a few of his well known finagles, was able to purchase a gasoline powered free flying model of his own. The kit he brought home required a .049 cu. in. engine and though smaller, was similar to Adam's plane, with a double dihedral wing. Harry carefully inspected his younger brother's selection then loaned Jimmy one of his older .049 engines to eliminate the issue of motor break in.

Jimmy's free flyer was called "The Star Duster, and he worked hard to assure his model's success. As always, Harry was close by to help his little brother and assure the newest aircraft in our neighborhood was built correctly in a relatively short amount of time. Jimmy selected a black and white color scheme for his ship and she stood out well against our blue Oregonian sky. Jimmy's free flyer turned out great and we couldn't wait for Harry to begin testing his younger brother's ship for flight.

Harry began by double checking the Star Duster's little engine in the hangar, then gave the aircraft his overall pre-flight inspection. Upon completion of our mentor's pre-flight ground check, everything was set and The Star Duster" was scheduled to fly the next morning.

We all got up early the next day, and headed to the hangar to help prepare for the maiden flight of Jimmy's free flyer. All of Jimmy's preparations went according to plan and we were on the flying field before dawn. Harry took over the usual pre-flight procedures and started the "Star Duster's motor for a warm up.

After what seemed to be an eternity, Harry gave the airplane to Jimmy, who immediately launched his model with all of his might. The Star Duster flew well and climbed in the sky according to plan. She rose several hundred feet when her fuel ran out, then gently glided to the ground for a soft landing. Jimmy's free flyer didn't suffer any damage and we all congratulated him for his successful efforts.

Gas powered control line aircraft was what we considered as the ultimate expression of skill in our approach to the hobby of model aviation. This appeal stemmed from the high level of construction those planes required, as well as the advanced degree of flying ability that control line aircraft demanded.

Our control line models were racers and had a corresponding price tag. Once again, we could only afford one of these kits per year and we wanted those kits to perform.

Fortunately, a lot of the cost of these control line kits could be saved by salvaging and transferring parts from past kits. One way or another we made do, and the three of us eventually became control line pilots.

Control line model aircraft models were very different from the other planes we flew. These models were designed and built to fly fast with robust controls for large, powerful engines. Our control line aircraft models were usually built from solid balsa fuselages with framed silk-span wings. These model planes were flown in circles and controlled by a U-shaped handle. One end of the handle was used for down elevator and the other end was used for the up elevator. Each of these control surfaces was attached to the control handle via a series of linkages accurately installed for precise racing applications. The linkages were then connected to nylon line that terminated in the handle itself. The rudder of the aircraft was offset 20 degrees to assume the correct centrifugal profile for a taut control line relationship between the pilot and aircraft.

The speed and centrifugal force associated with flying our control line models meant that a great deal of stress was

applied to the ship's airframes. The framing and structure of control line aircraft had to not only account for this centrifugal force, but also the pull of the model's bigger engines, as well as the added weight of the plane's on board accessories and controls.

Strength and the efficient application of materials were the two primary principles we utilized in building our control line kits. We also built our ships carefully to insure correct center of gravity and flight performance, while stalling, and other undesirable flight characteristics were built out of our control line models. The controls for elevation and centrifugal offset were meticulously crafted into these aircraft to assure racing caliber responses as they were piloted from the ground.

Control line racing was fun but it required skill to avoid disaster. As always, Harry was very helpful to the three of us with the selection, construction and piloting of these fast and responsive planes. First, Harry taught us to select a control line plane that was appropriate to our flying ability.

Next, he mentored Jimmy, Adam and I on how to effectively construct a fast control line racer which was light and strong enough to withstand the demands of control line flying.

Generally, we flew our control line models in two ways. Either via relaxed non- competitive flight or racing. Whichever way, the pilot had to concentrate and rely on advanced piloting skill to avoid the expense of a devastating crash.

Harry began our training to include long sessions of non-competitive control line flights where we learned to safely take off, land and operate, our control line kits without mishap. Only after this new, challenging and non-competitive type of flying was mastered were we allowed to race our planes against each other under Harry's watchful guidance. After long hours and countless laps, I finally felt prepared to race my plane.

The two races we conducted were designed from our own imaginations and officiated by Harry, while the remainder of our group rotated from pilot to ground crew depending on whose plane was racing. The first race consisted of a five lap sprint and the second was a twenty lap endurance race. These races taught Adam, Jimmy and me a lot about model aeronautics. Harry was continually available to assure we flew our planes safely and we all had a lot of fun challenging one another with our Control Line Models.

My first gasoline powered control line airplane was called the Ringmaster. It was a fantastic plane with a wingspan of 42 inches and a length of 24 and1/2 inches.

She was powered by a .35 cu. in. engine and was pretty fast. I decided to paint my plane purple with gold trim and she looked great. Harry's mentoring paid off. My control line flyer was built as well as she looked and I couldn't wait to get her into the air.

I recall my first experience racing my control line flyer. I had been control line flying, crash free, for several weeks, when I decided to race my model for the first time. We talked it over and decided to race The Ringmaster the next day.

Early the next morning, "The Four Aces of Elliott Avenue," set out for the pasture to see if my aircraft was as fast as I thought it would be. Harry stood outside the circle scribed by my planes flight path and readied his stopwatch after thoroughly checking my plane, I signaled to Adam to start the engine of my ship. The little .35 roared to life and my _Ringmaster_ took off. My plane jumped into the air and I ran her through several laps before I gave Harry the signal to start timing. She ran the sprint race well and Harry said I had a good time. I landed my control line flyer quickly to give her a once over. Everything was fine and I decided to test the endurance of my aircraft.

After completing the customary preflight procedures, I had Adam re- start my model. She fired right up and dashed into the air as before. My plane covered the required twenty laps easily and I flew her ten or so laps past the limit for good measure. I landed my plane with a profound sense of relief for avoiding a crash and was grateful for the praise I received from my friends. The Ringmaster proved to be quite a control line airplane and she made many more successful flights throughout that fantastic Oregon summer.

Adam also had built a gas powered control line model that flew quite well. His kit, The Nobler was a larger plane than my Ringmaster, sporting a wingspan of 50 and 1/2 inches, and a length of 38 and 1/2 inches. Like me, he decided to power his ship with a .35 cu. in. engine. This duplication was in the interest of competition to see if his Nobler was faster than my Ringmaster.

Adam had completed his control line model around the same time I had completed The Ringmaster. He painted his ship deep blue with white trim and she looked great. Harry said Adam had done a fine job of building his plane and Adam looked forward to testing The Nobler under racing conditions.

103

Harry had also worked with Adam, teaching him piloting skills and Adam caught on quickly. After a couple of weeks of flight training, Adam was ready to race his control line flyer. It was decided Adam would solo his ship the morning following his last training flight and we were all excited to see how well The Nobler could fly.

We met at the hangar early the next day, gathered Adam's gear, and went to the flying field. We decided to follow the same racing itinerary I followed previously with a sprint race being followed by an endurance competition. Harry took over as the official timer, while Jimmy and I assumed the roles of ground crew.

We gave The Nobler the once over to be sure everything was o.k. as Adam walked to the center of the circle designated for flying our aircraft. He raised his hand and signaled me to start the motor of his plane. Jimmy left the take off point to stand by Harry as I started Adam's engine without calamity and suddenly my friend's control line racer was in the air. Adam took a couple of practice laps, then signaled Harry to time his plane in a sprint race. Adams's plane was fast, but not as fast as my Ringmaster. Adam landed his plane after several unsuccessful attempts at beating my time. We looked over The Nobler for damage after landing and found she was o.k. We could see that Adam was disappointed in his ship's performance, but he didn't let it get him down and my friend proceeded to try the endurance race.

We took up our racing positions and after the usual preflight test, inspection and protocols The Nobler was in the air again. Adam's plane flew great; she beat my time for endurance racing, and flew a grand total of eighty laps as well.

This lap total was a new record for our control line planes and Adam felt that he had redeemed himself. We each congratulated Adam for his efforts and Harry bought the victory sodas.

Jimmy was nearly excluded from control line flying. This situation was due to his parent's concern that their youngest son might get hurt playing with those fast and powerful aircraft. However, Harry went to bat for his younger brother and promised to help Jimmy safely build and fly a control line aircraft. Their parents finally relented, giving Harry and Jimmy the green light to pool their money for the purchase of a kit the next day.

Harry selected Carl Goldberg's Trainee as Jimmy's first racer. It was a smaller and slower ship than those flown by Adam and myself, but was a sufficient challenge for Jimmy to build and fly. Jimmy's plane had a wingspan of 30 inches, a length of 28 inches, and its 049 cu. in. engine gave The Trainee enough power for beginning level racing.

With Harry's help, Jimmy's control line racer turned out to be a fantastic little plane, painted in a yellow and red color scheme. Harry taught his little brother the basics of control line racing the same way as he had taught Adam an myself, and soon Jimmy was flying his plane with little assistance from his older brother.

After several weeks of flight training and a few crashes, Harry thought Jimmy was ready to solo. We met at the hangar early the next day to help with Jimmy's gear and then headed to the pasture to take advantage of the still morning air. Adam was appointed ground crew, I manned the stopwatch while Harry stood behind his little brother to assist if the need arose.

After a thorough pre-flight inspection, Adam fueled and test ran the plane's engine. All was o.k. Adam then nodded to Harry and we all readied ourselves to fly the Trainee.

Harry gave us the go signal and Adam restarted the Trainee's .049 engine. The little motor hummed and Jimmy's plane shot to the sky while I timed the event. Jimmy handled his plane well and she flew several laps before running out of fuel. Harry helped his younger brother take her in carefully and the little red and yellow racer landed gently without catastrophe. Jimmy's solo gas powered control line flight was successful and his time was good, we each praised our youngest ace for his accomplishment as Harry beamed with pride.

My friends and I enjoyed model aircraft for several years with the helpful guidance of Harry, our mentor. He taught us many things and counseled us continually through the myriad of problems we had making our planes. Unfortunately, the fun we had building and flying model aircraft came to a sudden close a couple of years later when Harry enlisted into the Air Force. Adam, Jimmy and I felt helpless without Harry and our interest in model aviation waned. Yet, I will always recall with fondness those magnificent mornings flying our handmade aircraft during those golden Oregon summers.

Chapter 11

Hawthorne Pool

Hawthorne Pool was the number one recreational destination our group sought during those hot Medford summers. Our oasis was a full size aquatics center located inside a twenty acre city park, and about four miles from my house. We usually grouped up and rode our bikes to the pool after lunch and subsequent to the completion of our chores. We would swim and play for hours, then peddle home as fast as we could to be on time for supper. I can still recollect that shady park and the fun we had playing in Hawthorne's refreshing waters.

The City of Medford operated one Olympic size swimming pool and one well appointed wading pool. Hawthorn Park usually opened the third week of June and closed the second week of August. The large pool featured one meter and three meter diving boards.

Life guards were always on duty to assure safety, and injuries were rare in our city's aquatic center.

All of the members of my group enjoyed swimming. However, Adam, Duane, Spencer, Heath and I were the ones who saved our money and paid the six dollars for season tickets.

Those passes were wonderful and allowed us to enjoy Hawthorne Pool any day of the week. It was fantastic to be able to swim and cool off when the weather got hot and the torrid dog days of summer sun began to beat down.

There were a lot of activities to get involved with at our aquatics center. Beginning and advanced swimming lessons, beginning and advanced diving lessons and lifeguard training, made Hawthorne Pool a busy place with lots of opportunity.

Generally, the classes lasted approximately one hour a day for a week and were free to those who possessed season tickets making them ideal to suit the needs of energetic young boys.

I recall one summer when the five of us decided to enroll in the swimming and diving courses offered by the pool.

Heath and Spencer gravitated to the swimming classes while Duane Adam and I preferred the diving class.

Heath first enrolled in the intermediate swimming class then was quickly advanced according to his ability. Adam, Duane, and I also decided to sign up for the intermediate swimming class then our attention gravitated to the beginning diving class. Spencer was placed in the beginning swimming course in order to learn to swim, a vital prerequisite to graduate from the wading pool to the full sized pool.

We had a lot of fun with those classes and learned a lot from the expert instruction.

We recognized Heath as our pool leader. This exalted position was awarded to him after his heroic lifesaving effort the year before and we each looked to our leader as our personal lifeguard. Fortunately, Heath didn't let this boyish fanfare go to his head and conducted himself with his usual soft spoken aplomb.

Heath immediately displayed his love of the water in the intermediate swimming class and with minor instruction, was moved to the advanced course where his ability was challenged to a greater degree. In time, Heath became an excellent swimmer and advanced in his age group rankings quickly. Eventually, he was invited to practice with the club swim team, and had acquired a degree of renown around our city pool. My friend usually won the majority of the races conducted for his age group and placed well in several events conducted for competitors older than he was. Heath later went on to be a High School champion and swam at the collegiate level.

The events Heath loved the most were the fifty yard freestyle and the one hundred yard freestyle.

It was exciting to go to those meets and watch one of my closest friends be so successful.

It was also refreshing to witness Heath take his new found fame in stride, preferring to hang around with our group in favor of the fans he had suddenly gained.

Duane, Adam, and I were also enrolled for intermediate level swimming program, but got bored with lap training.

We began to wonder if this whole aquatics thing was something we wanted to do, then transferred to diving class. The three of us immediately took to diving and decided the Hawthorne Pool recreational program was worthwhile after all.

My friends and I had a lot of fun learning to dive at that wonderful Park. The three of us had our share of occasional wipe outs, but we still had a lot of fun. As beginners, we were taught exclusively from the low board. We learned to adjust the tension of the board to achieve the most bounce, and how to perform a controlled approach. We also learned to perform a complete dive called a half from the forward and backward position.

After graduating from beginning diving instruction, we progressed to the intermediate diving class. We still were training solely on the low board, and things began to get real interesting as we learned how to time and execute our diving stunts for a splashless entry. We moved on to mastering full forward and backward flips and felt confident to go on to the advanced segment of the diving program.

The advanced diving class was considerably harder and required more concentration. We finally were moved to the high board where we spent a considerable amount of time reviewing and refining our approaches from the height of ten feet.

We also learned how to execute a swan dive and advance our flips to a one and a half from the high board.

I recall one warm summer morning when Heath, Adam, and myself decided to enter one of the swim meets offered by our city pool. Duane couldn't decide if he wanted to compete and Spencer couldn't enter the meet due to his young age. Adam and I knew we couldn't keep up with Heath, so we concentrated our efforts on the diving competition. Duane eventually became disinterested in both the swimming and diving competitions and preferred to loll on the pool deck talking to girls. Spencer tagged along and pestered his older brother by interfering with his flirtations and being a general nuisance.

My closest friend and I became embroiled in the diving contest as Heath was overwhelming the swimming competition single handed. Adam's specialty was diving from the low board, while I had become proficient at diving from the high board. We each could dive and perform forward as well as backward flips, from our selected rostrums and were ready to see how we could contend in open competition.

The diving competition was begun on the low board with the judge first calling for a forward half to be executed by all the contestants. There were about ten boys in the competition and both Adam and I knew we had to be good to win. We executed our first dives well and were ready to proceed in the contest.

The low board event progressed and several competitors had already wiped out when both Adam and I came to the concluding segment of the one meter competition. This event was the dreaded back flip, and Adam performed his dive effortlessly. I was called to perform next, but my back flip wasn't as good as Adam's and I wound up being relegated to second place.

After concluding the low board challenge, we went on to the three meter portion of the diving competition. We immediately noticed the large number of spectators who had filled the bleachers around the diving end of the pool. Adam and I knew this audience wasn't there to witness our diving expertise, but to revel at our subsequent humiliation after wiping out.

The itinerary for the three meter competition was identical to that of the one meter competition with both Adam and I moving ahead in the contest rapidly. After completing our preliminary dives, we went on to perform our flips. Adam went first and wiped out hitting the water with a dramatic belly flop.

The crowd went wild, laughing and pointing at Adam while shouting derisive remarks. Adam took this ridicule well and ignored the negative atmosphere he had accidentally created.

Now it was my turn. I noticed the crowd quieted down as I climbed the ladder. I walked to the end of the board in eerie silence, and then pivoted into position.

I said to myself, "this is it," then simultaneously jumped and flipped, landing in the water feet first without error.

I was a success and took home the blue ribbon for our age group in the high dive. Adam took home the blue ribbon for our age group in the low dive.

We were proud of those ribbons and were showing them off to anybody we thought was interested when Heath appeared with his long accumulation of awards. Suddenly, it was all too clear who the undisputed champion of Hawthorne Pool really was.

My friends and I greatly enjoyed our oasis in the middle of Hawthorne Park. The arboreal surroundings invited, the pool refreshed, and we learned a great deal from the marvelous aquatic program offered by the City of Medford. I'll never forget the fun we had splashing, swimming, diving and evading the heat, at our shady pool during the golden Oregonian summers of my youth.

Chapter 12

Athletics

The athletic programs offered by the City of Medford and the Medford School District were superior. The sports offered within those programs helped to develop me into a collegiate level athlete and shaped my life for many years to come.

Medford's athletic agenda began with a summer recreationally oriented list of sports, offered to kids by the City of Medford ranging from grade school through high school level. These sports included tennis, swimming, diving, track and little league baseball. Everyone was invited to compete and the winners were awarded trophies, medals, or ribbons, depending upon their sport and ability. There were several age group divisions for boys as well as girls and it was great fun.

Medford's schools formally offered a list of competitive athletics that were well organized and lasted throughout the school year.

Unfortunately the sports offered by the Medford School District at this time were primarily male only, as this was the late 1950's and Title 9 was over a decade from fruition.

Medford School Athletics began at the elementary level. The primary facilities were excellent with each school having its own football and baseball fields as well as gyms. The equipment provided was also top notch to afford each participant the safest and best opportunity to succeed. Professional physical educators were placed in every school as P. E. Trainers and coaches to assure correct development and a proper approach to each sport. Referees and sports officials were also a mandatory part of every contest to guarantee sportsmanship and fair play.

The elementary school athletic program enlisted eight schools and featured four sports. This program was well thought through and featured cheer leaders as well as city wide championships, for the schools within the district. Participation was begun in the fourth grade and included football, basketball, baseball, and track and field. Athletes were discovered at this level then groomed to continue in their chosen sports within the programs of their respective junior high schools.

The junior high athletic program consisted of two schools and added wrestling as the fifth sport to be offered. League play was begun at this level and our junior high teams competed against other junior high teams from Grants Pass and Ashland.

Medford's junior high home contests were played on the high school fields, some at night and under the lights that added an aura of wonder to the uninitiated. Equipment, cheerleaders, coaching, officiating, facilities and transportation were copiously provided to assure an excellent experience for those interested in athletics.

The Medford High School's sports program was the top step in the ladder of athletics offered by the Medford Public Schools. This program was renown throughout the State of Oregon and reflected the best competitors the city had to offer.

Athletes such as John Fosbury (Olympic Gold Medalist) and Bill Enyart (Oakland Raiders and New England Patriots) are two of the more renowned graduates of Medford's excellent program of athletics. Medford's sports program included football, basketball, baseball, as well as track and field, tennis, swimming and wrestling. Each sport was designed to be a showcase of excellence for what the city offered. The facilities were first class, the equipment excellent and the experience fulfilling. The athletic events were backed by the entire town and I still recall going to see the Medford High School Black Tornadoes and witnessing that magnificent athletic atmosphere as a boy.

Duane, Reuben, and I had many great experiences as we progressed in Medford's Athletic Program. The three of us were the same age and played on many of the same teams, enduring losses, learning valuable lessons in addition to savoring wins while we grew as athletes. However, it was the sports we played and the experiences we had in elementary school that I recall most fondly.

117

My first meaningful athletic experience occurred in the sport of football when my Howard School Mustangs took the field against one of our cross town rivals. This game was between the sixth grade level teams of each school and not the best example of grid iron play. Yet, we had fun and I was the starting fullback.

Our team had memorized the plays of our play book and felt confident we could crush any opposition sent in our direction. We began our season by winning the coin toss and our coach decided to receive the ball from the opening kick-off.

The kick was actually a pass thrown by the referee and after first fumbling, then recovering our return, we found ourselves on our own ten yard line. We attempted a pass play without success and the forty spinner play was called. This was the play where I received the ball and ran straight up the middle. It worked, and I ran for a ninety yard touchdown. I couldn't believe what happened and everyone gathered round to congratulate me.

My brief moment of glory was fleeting and it didn't take long for me to be relieved of my false sense of pride.

Our team was playing defense on the next series of downs and I was positioned as safety. Coach Collie had repeatedly told me a good safety never lets anybody get behind him and that I was the last man on the team to defend our goal. My coach's edicts stuck in my mind and I thought I had everything under control when the end from the Stars somehow got behind me and scored. Suddenly I was no longer the hero but the goat as my feelings of shame extinguished the pride I once possessed.

This situation taught me the valuable lessons that glory is never constant and that I should never rest on my laurels.

Another of my sports memories occurred the following spring when I first became involved with the sport of track and field. My mentor had observed my jumping ability through the year in Football as well as Basketball and suggested I compete in the High Jump event. I was eager and soon was doggedly practicing to leap over the bar at a moderate height

I began at the three foot mark, then progressed to three inches, and with my mentor's benevolent guidance was clearing the three feet 6 inch mark regularly.

The following day at practice, my coach suggested I needed more of a challenge and raised the bar to three feet, eight inches. This was daunting and the record height for fourth grade high jumpers at our school. I immediately began to balk and make excuses but Mr. Collie was firm and assured success. I cleared the bar on my second attempt and was very proud. Coach Collie praised me and said I had done well in practice, but that I needed to prove myself the following Friday at our meet versus Hoover Elementary.

I trained hard all week and could not wait for that fateful day to arrive. My mentor had prepared me well, instilling confidence while dismissing false pride. The high jump competition went on without a hitch until the bar was raised to the three feet, eight inch measure. I made several attempts at that height but failed on all three tries. I was frustrated and didn't understand why I failed in my official record attempts yet was successful in my unofficial practice attempts for the identical standard.

My predicament continued for several more weeks. I worked hard and increasingly succeeded with my practice three feet, eight inch jumps, only to repeatedly fail when the bar was raised to the identical height in meet competition. I couldn't figure out what was wrong and the track season was coming to a close with only the All City Track Meet left for official competition.

My coach had witnessed my dilemma and sat me down the day before the final meet of the year. Mr. Collie told me that my problem was in my head, and to let things flow.

I listened intently to my coach's words and said I would try again tomorrow.

I thought about my coach's advice all night and came to realize he was right. All I had to do was to perform at the meet in the same way I performed in practice. Now I was truly ready and couldn't wait for the final meet of my sixth grade year to begin.

The Elementary School All City Track Meet was conducted at the High School Stadium on a beautiful Saturday morning in late May. The high jump competition went flawlessly for me and I went on to set a new school record of three feet, ten inches. I was elated when everyone praised me, and could not wait to tell Coach Collie.

I still recall the broad smile on my mentor's face as he approached and shook my hand. I looked up into his kind and guiding face and listened expectantly for his pearls of wisdom. My Coach looked me squarely in the eye and with a sudden expression of determination spoke the phrase millions of coaches have said since sports began, "Now let's quit horsing around and get to work."

This event proved useful to me as a young athlete for several reasons. It taught me the value of perseverance, the linkage of a proper mindset to succeed as well as the significance of sound advice.

These values served me well through the years and I will never forget my Coaches sound advice.

My baseball experience also began as a Howard School Mustang. I still remember the fun we had at the games while the sights and smells of spring permeated my senses. My friends and I were developing into a pretty good group of Elementary School level baseball players who could hit with authority, play in a coordinated manner and run the bases quickly.

One series of events stands out in my memory from that golden Baseball season so long ago. These misfortunate episodes concerned my abysmal batting slump and unfolded as my team progressed through the spring. Auspiciously, my bat finally came around at the end of our sixth grade league baseball championship game against another elementary level baseball team. We had participated in our example of the national pastime throughout the spring and won our share of the contests. Duane had become a pretty good pitcher and was throwing a lot of strike outs while Reuben was using his bat with authority, knocking in home runs on a regular basis. Unfortunately, my baseball skills hadn't progressed as well as my teammates. I was having trouble at the plate and was striking out more than I was getting hits.

Coach Collie said I wasn't keeping my eye on the ball and that I should be more selective of the pitches offered me.

I took my coach's advice to heart and worked hard at eyeing the pitches offered me while concentrating on hitting the ball.

As the season progressed my batting improved and I was feeling more confident at the plate. Mr. Collie had continued to emphasize ball concentration and pitch selectivity every time I got up to bat. My Coaches insistent prodding helped and I felt well prepared by the time our elementary league baseball championship arrived.

We met to play our adversaries on our own baseball field one warm day in mid April. Our opposition had a boy named Rocky who was a pretty good athlete and known to be a good hitter.

Duane pitched to him well and the score was tied at three runs going to the bottom of the ninth inning. Heath, and Adam, had struck out and I was due up with two outs. I was approaching the plate when Coach Collie called me aside and instructed me to be selective of the opposing pitcher's offerings and to watch the ball into my bat. I had taken two balls and one strike when the pitcher delivered the pitch I had been waiting for. The ball flew over home plate in the center of the strike zone and I clobbered it. I can still recollect seeing that ball fly into the barrel of my bat as I swung and made solid contact. The next thing I knew the ball was going over the right field fence giving my team the league championship victory.

I ran the bases and felt like Roger Maris, when my teammates all gathered to pat me on the back as I crossed home plate

After my triumph, I went to my mentor in search of approval. Mr. Collie congratulated me when I got to the bench and inspired me by saying, "Making the right choices in life is also important and to always select my options carefully." I never forgot the valuable life lesson I received from my coach during that long past golden spring and I still concentrate on the selected things I value in life to this day.

My friend Duane, also enjoyed sports and developed into quite an athlete during those formative years at Howard Elementary. He had a good eye, was a fast runner, and possessed an unusual amount of stamina that Mr. Collie eagerly utilized. Under our coach's guidance, Duane became the quarterback on the football team, the point guard on the basketball team and our star distance runner on the track team.

To this day I am reminded of Duane's first test in sports. That ordeal occurred during a cool fall afternoon on our elementary school's football field. My friend had been working hard on his passing since the season began and we all felt confident in our passing attack. Duane's test came during the second game of our fifth grade season against a challenger from the east side of town. We hadn't been running the ball very well against our opposition when Coach Collie signaled for one of our passing plays to be executed. Duane called the play in the huddle that required Adam, our split end, to streak down the sideline, catch Hawkeye's pass and score an expected touchdown. We looked to the sideline to be sure of our coach's choice and eyed the determined expression on our mentor's face, then expectantly lined up on the ball. My friends nodded to one another with affirmation then executed a failed version of the called play with an interception being the result.

After we returned to the sidelines, coach looked at Duane disapprovingly then stated, "You're a better athlete than that."

123

I could see the intense embarrassment reflected on Hawkeye's face and saw my friend was feeling dejected. I immediately gathered Reuben, Heath, and Adam, as well as the other members of our team, and we went to console Duane.

Following our team's impromptu pep talk, we all agreed to improve and play at a more successful level of performance.

Our team was able to stop our rival's offense following Hawkeye's interception and Mr. Collie called another pass play to be implemented when we took the field. We felt confident of our coach's play selection as we lined up in our respective positions. Once again Adam and Duane nodded to one another in confirmation and the play was executed flawlessly when Adam caught Duane's pass and crossed the goal line without being touched. Immediately we congratulated our two heroes and Duane's fifth grade football season was off to a good start.

This athletic episode was valuable to me for several reasons. Duane's trial educated me in the importance of positive support during times of struggle. My friend's ordeal also illustrated to me the value of teamwork in a time of crisis and that nobody can successfully endure life's trials alone.

Duane also excelled in basketball and earned the captaincy of our elementary school team. Hawkeye was a good ball handler as well as a great shooter and his skills earned our team a lot of basketball victories.

Duane had several memorable games, yet the first contest we had in my sixth grade year was the game I remember as most meaningful.

This competitor always seemed to have the best elementary school basketball teams in town and usually trounced everyone they faced year after year.

We felt this situation was going to abruptly change when they came to our gym one dreary December afternoon.

From the start of the contest everyone thought this was going to be our game. Hawkeye was a dominating figure both offensively and defensively. Offensively, he was handling the ball exceptionally well, passing or dribbling through our rival's defense and scoring regularly. Defensively, he disrupted our challenger's guards and stole or intercepted the ball repeatedly. My friend's performance was amazing to watch, and even Coach Collie admitted he was having a great day .

Everything was rolling along and our foes looked to be finished when Reuben unpredictably twisted his ankle and had to leave the game early in the third quarter.

Our coach called a time out and told Duane that the game was on his shoulders. Our team commended Duane and cheered Coach Collie's decision in affirmation.

Hawkeye told us, "Were going to win this game and to get to work."

We took the court with confidence, but it became immediately apparent that things were going to change for the worse. We weren't getting the rebounds we did when Reuben was playing and Duane began to push his shots and pass erratically. Our adversaries immediately took advantage and gradually took control of the game. Duane attempted to confront the competitor's onslaught singlehandedly by coordinating our offense and passing the ball as best he could to whoever he could. Unfortunately, my friend's efforts were for naught as our team's capabilities were dramatically curtailed without the Howard School colossus. Gradually Duane's offensive and defensive options became increasingly limited without Reuben and our team couldn't counter our competitor juggernaut. The third and fourth quarters dragged on and we ended up losing to our challenger by fifteen points. Duane was severely discouraged after the loss and felt our team's failure was his fault. Our basketball squad consoled Duane after the game and my friend pulled out of his doldrums shortly afterward.

We met again later that same year in our conference basketball championship game and cruised to an easy win via teamwork with Reuben and our emotionally restored captain leading the way.

Our first sixth grade basketball game was not only memorable but very meaningful to me for two reasons. I witnessed how my friend had erred by irrevocably coming to over-anticipate the glory of defeating our opponent on that winter afternoon. I also observed the abject depression my friend experienced when his expectations of victory weren't met. This experience and its aftermath taught me the dangers of over expectation and never to put the cart before the horse.

Duane also excelled in track as a distance runner. He had a remarkable amount of stamina and always posted the fastest times in the six hundred yard dash when we raced for time in physical education class. Coach Collie realized Hawkeye's talent early and recruited my friend as a distance runner for our elementary school track team. Duane's ability was groomed over the next two years and by the time he was in the sixth grade, he had become the best six hundred yard dash runner in our town for elementary level competitors.

Our sixth grade track team had beaten everyone we faced in dual meet competition. However, one group of Elementary harriers was giving us a strong challenge at our league track championships.

Our team was tied with our antagonists and everything had come down to the six hundred yard dash.

Hawkeye was assigned the inside lane, a standard reward for his consistent string of victories in the event during the regular Track and Field season. Everyone on our team was getting nervous when Coach Collie took us aside and skillfully calmed us with soothing words. We quickly settled down and began to cheer for our champion harrier. Every member of our team had their eyes fixed on the race when the competitors were called to the starting line. I could see my friend was ready for this test and was going to turn in a great time.

The race was close at first, but Duane took the lead at the half way point and then strode off to easily win the race by five yards. It was wonderful, and we gratefully mobbed our hero after he crossed the finish line.

This incident taught me the paradigm of seizing the moment and to always achieve as best you can when one is placed in an enviable situation.

Reuben was easily the best athlete of our group. He was well coordinated, a very fast runner, and nearly two feet taller as well as fifty pounds heavier than anybody in the Medford area for his age. Reuben was a force of nature who became very skilled in football, basketball, as well as track and field.

Our athletic teams perpetually relied on him to triumph and we won many elementary school level contests due to his gigantic presence. Reuben later went on to star as an athlete at our junior high and high school, ultimately earning an athletic scholarship to a major university.

In elementary school football, Reuben dominated wherever the coaches decided to position him. The Howard School Titan began his elementary school football experience at the position of center, then tackle, and finally at tight end. As a tight end he was unstoppable and scored touchdown after touchdown, usually accompanied by several unsuccessful tacklers whom he carried over the goal line.

I recall our sixth grade championship game against another elementary school football squad. . This contest set the stage for a dramatic display of my colossal friend's athleticism and hinted to everyone in attendance what was to come in the future.

Our elementary level football championship began on a cool fall Friday afternoon at our home field.

We were facing a tough opponent and knew their team was going to be a challenge. Our rival had quickly run the ball for a touchdown, then intercepted a pass and scored again. Suddenly, we were down fourteen points and wondering what happened.Once again, Coach Collie came to the rescue and calmed us with soothing words.

That speech worked and soon we were back to normal. Coach Collie called for Duane to pass to our tight end, Reuben. The pass was completed and Reuben easily scored.

Coach called that play all afternoon and Reuben delivered by scoring nine touchdowns in that game. The oposing team couldn't stop him and he literally looked like a man amongst boys as he repeatedly ran through their defense.

Offensively, Reuben was amazing, yet he stood out on the defensive side of the ball as well. Coach Collie put our colossus on the defensive line against our foe where they soon found he couldn't be blocked. Our adversaries would repeatedly attempt to double team or triple team Reuben, only to witness the Howard School hulk casting each assailant aside and tackling the ball carrier for a loss. If our rival passed, Reuben would knock the ball down, or grab it from the air to score one of his three defensive touch downs. Our man mountain proved to be a complete, inexorable power on the defensive side of the ball and our opponents didn't score another point.

The final score of our elementary school league championship was favored our team by the margin of 84 to 14. Every point we scored was by Reuben, as there was no kicking involved and touchdowns were assessed at seven points each.

Several junior high school coaches were in attendance to witness our triumph against Wilson. They had learned of my friend's size in addition to his ability and wanted to see if he was the real thing. We could see the middle school staff was impressed while we cheered to celebrate our gargantuan teammate's amazing performance.

This experience was one of the many stupendous performances I witnessed as Reuben's teammate. Yet, this 84 point performance against a familiar challenger, more than any other, taught me how valuable strength, size and ability can be in an athletic contest.

Another sport where Reuben excelled was basketball. Here too, his six feet plus height and two hundred plus pound frame made him the irresistible force who led us to our elementary league basketball championship.

Reuben played center on the opposing basketball team. Coach Collie constantly worked with him and my colossal friend had become a skilled basketball player by the time he was in the sixth grade. Offensively, he learned to successfully position himself to take a pass, and then efficiently take the ball to the rim and score. Defensively, Coach taught him the art of blocking shots and rebounding to complete his elementary level basketball resume.

The game we played for our school's elementary basketball championship was against Wilson Elementary. We had previously been beaten by Wilson that year and were spoiling for revenge.

The game was played in pour rival's gym on a cold winter morning in early January. Coach Collie prepared us well, Reuben was ready and our team was focused on the task at hand.

The game started with our opponents getting a good lead. Our opponents gaurd had shut down Duane's shooting when Coach Collie called a time out to settle everybody down. Our mentor told us to stick to our game strategy of setting up on offense and letting Hawkeye get the ball to Reuben as he posted up at center. Defensively, he told our colossus to block every shot he could and to go after every rebound.

From that point, Reuben put on an exhibition of scoring, rebounding, and shot blocking akin to what I had seen of Wilt Chamberlain on television. His performance was amazing .

Reuben scored thirty points, had five blocked shots and we beat our antagonists by twenty points.

After the game, we surrounded and cheered our gargantuan hero, along with several coaches from the junior high program who had been coming to see the Howard School Titan on a regular basis. Each coach showered my friend with flattering tributes, stating Reuben had a bright future and that they couldn't wait to enroll him in their program when the time arrived. This was my first experience with athletic recruiting and I found it moderately repulsive. I felt the junior high school coaches whom I respected from afar were somewhat phony and excessive up close with a prattle that lay emphasis on winning at all cost. This experience was surprising to me and I retained it in my memory, recalling its unpleasant details when I was recruited for collegiate football some years later.

Track and field was another sport that favored Reuben's size and strength. The shot put was the event he favored the most, and Reuben showed promise from the beginning. I still recall with amazement how far he could launch that iron ball, and the ease with which he completed his throws.

Reuben's career in track began in the fourth grade where our coach quickly began to prepare my friend for competition.

Coach Collie had already witnessed my gigantic friend's extraordinary dimension and ability in football as well as basketball and felt our school's Goliath had a bright future in the weight events.

Coach was right — Reuben unofficially topped the school record for sixth grade level Shot Putting the very first time he threw a shot as a fourth grade competitor.

Moreover, he went on to crush the city records for seventh and eighth grade level Shot Put tossing in that same track season.

Reuben was awesome to watch as his colossal frame entered the shot putting ring and he effortlessly outdistanced the competition. We could always count on my huge friend to win his events and his enormous presence gave our elementary school track team the impetus for victory.

Unfortunately, Reuben's boundless talent in track and field was not well received by everyone in the Medford athletic community. In fact, my friend's prodigious size and abilities provoked some to demand he be barred from all sporting events. This unsavory situation came to the fore the week of our Elementary level, "All- City Championship Meet. This was the week that the complaint demanding Reuben be excluded from all district athletic competitions due to his extraordinary dimension and talent was heard.

A meeting was called to be held after school and attended by the parties involved. At first, I was amazed at the demands made by the plaintiffs against my buddy. Then, for the first time I became aware of how hurtful jealousy and hate can be.

Coach Collie counseled our team on the issue and told us to support our gigantic friend. We took our mentor's advice to heart and supported Reuben with the true spirit of friendship and camaraderie.

Fortunately, Reuben's affair with isolation did not last and the silly and hurtful claim against my gigantic comrade was promptly dismissed. Reuben was allowed to compete that same week against the hateful antagonists who had attempted to derail his athletic experience.

Once again our Howard School Colossus demonstrated its phenomenal abilities, winning the Shot Put event as he took things in stride with a level head and malice toward none.

After the meet, our coach told us we should be very grateful for having a teammate such as Reuben and to put this unfortunate incident behind us. We instantly responded and gave our friend several loud and proud cheers of support.

I was especially uplifted by Reuben for the way he responded to his predicament and how he handled himself during this time of crisis.

Reuben managed his unexpected glory well. He approached his newfound fame with level headed aplomb, taking his numerous accolades in stride. Our Howard School Goliath just wanted to be one of the gang and not regarded as a standout.

Unfortunately, Reuben's desire to be a regular guy was not in his future. The more he succeeded athletically, the more he distanced himself from anonymity. As I observed my large friend's athletic experience, I witnessed this irony developing in his life. All Reuben really wanted was to be regarded as ordinary, yet his extraordinary size and athleticism continually pushed him into being regarded as an anatomical oddity and somebody quite abnormal. Ultimately, I viewed Reuben's paradox with sadness as I knew my gargantuan comrade would have preferred the social aspects of his life to have evolved in a more obscure and less dramatic manner.

The sports I played at Howard School Elementary were extremely influential. This athletic influence gave me confidence, a sense of accomplishment and an appreciation for camaraderie and taught me many lessons useful in life. Those elementary level sports were especially significant as the athletic experiences they provided were my first and most powerful.

Chapter 13

Push Car Racing

Push car racing was an activity my friends and I got captivated with one late spring. This infatuation began on a sunny Saturday afternoon at the local theater when we were initially exposed to the Soap Box Derby via a special feature shown on the movie house screen. The brightly painted cars, the galleries of fans and most importantly, the huge trophy presented to the winner of the race enthralled every member of our group. Each of us immediately began to imagine constructing individual race cars to enter and compete against one other in our own Soap Box Derby.

My friends and I eagerly talked up the idea of having our own version of a Soap Box Derby while we made our way home from the theater that same afternoon. Immediately several problems came to mind as we fantasized about racing our own home made cars. First, the real Soap Box Derby had always been conducted as a downhill race.

In contrast, our nearest hill, Roxy Ann Peak, was nearly ten miles away, creating an enormous logistical problem of transporting our proposed cars as well as ourselves to that distant site. Next, the construction of the race cars was going to be problematic due to the materials and hardware required in addition to their associated cost. We also were going to need help building our cars, as Seth and Harry, the eldest members of our group, weren't interested in our car racing enterprise whatsoever.

As we talked we decided to alter the format of the original Soap Box Derby and hold our race on a flat course. We resolved to utilize the level access road behind my grandparent's pasture as the track for our contest.

The race was initially to be conducted as a one lap enterprise beginning at a point marked as the starting line and proceeding to a point established as the mid-point then concluding by turning 180 degrees and racing back to the starting point.

Our start/finish line was intended to be marked by a line we drew in the road parallel with the posts of the south gate to our pasture. The mid-point of our homemade racetrack was a hay bale we planned to place in the center of the road approximately one hundred feet north from the start/finish line and aligned with one of the standpipes of my Grandparent's grazing land.

Our flat track race required two-man teams to be established for each vehicle with one team member being the driver and the other team member being the pusher. This situation also required both driver and pusher to rotate their positions in a fair manner as nobody wanted to be continually relegated to pushing one of our cars continually throughout a race. We decided to have each team rotate positions at the hay bale marking the mid-point of the race thereby giving each team member an equal share of driving and pushing.

My friends and I decided to establish four teams of racers who would each build and race their representative car. Adam and I would comprise one team, Spencer and Reuben made up another team, the third team consisted of Duane and Jimmy while Heath and Matt enlisted as the fourth team. These teams were far from perfect in equivalence but were adequate for our needs and besides the teams could always be adjusted in later races for fairness.

As our homeward discussion continued, we talked about the problems of building our race cars. Where were we to get the materials we would need to build the sturdy racers required for our derby? How much were these necessities going to cost? Who was going to help us build our push cars?

We thought as we pedaled and then I got the idea to go to my grandfather for help. My grampa was a former motorcycle racer as well as a stunt rider and he was a mechanic. Who better to ask for help building our race cars? We all agreed and decided to seek help from my elder patriarch when he arrived home from work.

Later that day, my friends and I gathered in my front yard to ask my grandfather for assistance in building our push cars.

We talked things over for a final time then entered my house in search of the assistance we sorely needed. My grampa knew something was up when all eight of us entered his living room en masse. He looked us over, calmly lit his cigarette and said, "let's have it." He obviously expected to hear a tale of sorrow for some mishap we had caused. We pleaded our case and then stood transfixed, waiting for my grandfather's response. Suddenly, my grampa beamed with delight and said he would be happy to help us build our push cars. Next, he asked what we were going to build our cars with. Upon hearing our unwitted response my grandfather said he would talk to a couple of his friends down town and arrange for the lumber and hardware we would need. He then advised us that we could get started sometime the following week as it would take a couple of days to get the required materials and the permission from the parents of those intending to race. My grandfather then asked where we planned to hold our push car race. We told him that the first Elliott Road push car derby was going to be held in the access road behind our pasture.

My grampa's enthusiasm quickly waned when he heard our reply. He looked worried, then frowned and reluctantly approved the site for our race. Everything was set and my friends and I gave my grandfather a big cheer.

We were thrilled as our last three major push car racing problems were solved. We were going to get the expert help we needed to build our cars, the expensive materials we required were going to be made available and it wasn't going to cost us a penny thanks to my wonderful grampa.

The days passed slowly while my friends and I waited for the materials we needed to complete our push cars. It seemed like we spent all our time talking and planning about our version of the Soap Box Derby as we lingered in anticipation for those valuable supplies.

One evening, a topic arose that concerned every member of our self appointed racing committee: trophies. What was to be the award for the winner of our grand race? Would the triumphant driver get a ribbon, a medal or perhaps a loving cup? Where would we get one of those prizes? How much would it cost? These were enormous problems for a group of ten year old boys to grapple with. Suddenly, the answer came to me. We could utilize one of the old trophies my grandfather had won years before and were unceremoniously stashed in the back of our car port. This idea was the perfect solution to our award search. The victor of our race would receive a large golden loving cup and it would be free thanks to my brilliant idea. There was only one problem left to deal with; getting my grandfather's permission to use one of his cups for the victory trophy of our push car race.

I felt confident about asking my grampa for one of his trophies for two reasons. First, I knew my grandmother had been pestering him about the storage space those tarnished ornaments occupied. Second, I felt my grandfather's sudden and dramatic interest in our race would tip the scales of fate my way and my grampa would acquiesce to my request.

That evening after dinner I asked my grampa if my friends and I could have one of his old loving cups to use as a prize for winning our push car race. My hunch was right and my grandfather quickly consented to my request.

He said to me, "Take whichever one of those old dust catchers that pleases you."

Immediately, I went into our carport and began to go through the large stash of trophies my kind old patriarch had offered. There were several candidates available and

141

some of those victory cups stood as tall as I was. I finally selected the brightest and shiniest cup available. It was nearly five feet high, decorated with gold and silver checkered flags and had a motorcycle on top that I chose to ignore in favor of its other attributes.

I pulled out the old loving cup, shined it up and showed it to my fellow racers the next morning. My friends loved and admired that old trophy and it was unanimously established as the grand trophy for the Elliott Road Soap Box Derby.

My grandfather delivered the lumber and hardware for our push-cars later that week. After dinner, my friends and I made ourselves available to unload the precious materials into my grampa's spacious shop. After all the materials were neatly placed we turned to our experienced racing consultant for further instructions.

My grandfather looked over everything carefully then walked to his workbench and we closely surrounded him as he drew the plans for our racing vehicles. He told us he thought we should race a modified version of the original Soap Box Derby racers. These cars would have a hood only to save weight and were designed to include a sophisticated brake and steering system for safety. My grandfather also informed us there was only one set of plans needed for our cars because they were going to be identical in length, width and wheelbase. This uniformity made my friends and me uneasy at first, but he said it was the only way to make things fair for everybody and that it was the way they did things at the Indianapolis 500. Eventually, we agreed and the work on our cars began in earnest.

My grandfather began the construction of our Elliott Road Derby racers by giving each racing team a job responsibility. Adam and I cut the 2x4s for the cars frames, Reuben and Spencer worked on the axles and the wheels, Duane and Jimmy cut the wood for our chariots hoods while Heath and Matt worked on the general constrution of the cars. Ultimately, my Grandfather oversaw the entire process and handled the more difficult assemblies.

The two push car components my grampa paid special attention to were the steering and brake assemblies. He designed and built each of these mechanisms identically for each of our four race cars with ingenious skill to produce a remarkable level of operational control.

The brake assemblies of our push cars consisted of a rake bolted into position inside a bracketed steel collar mounted ahead of the rear axle. This bracket assembly positioned the rake handle to continue from the tines through the collar to a neutral catch located next to the driver's seat.

The mechanism permitted the driver to apply his brakes by releasing the neutral catch while griping the rake handle then lifting up. The amount of applied braking power was governed by the driver and was equivalent to how hard he pulled up on the rake handle. This application of force was mechanically transferred to braking power via the fulcrum and lever relationship of the rake handle's bracket point and its association with the driver's grip point. Stopping power became available when the driver raised the handle of the rake and the tines of the tool correspondingly dug into the road surface just ahead and below the push car's rear axle. My grandfather's light weight, efficient and simple braking system worked well and significantly enhanced the control of our push cars without failing.

My friends and I first attempted to solve the problem of directing our push cars with the simple rope pull system commonly used in neighborhood push cars.

This idea was quickly dismissed as unsafe by my grandfather, who chose instead to fabricate the steering parts of our vehicles himself.

He copied the all steel mechanism used in go carts and utilized steering shafts, pitman arms, tie rods and spindles to guarantee a safe method of steering our derby racers. Once again my grampa's mechanical skill paid off and our rudimentary racers maneuvered through turns like Indy specials.

My grampa's assistance assured the construction of our cars was off to a great start and by the end of the first week a few of my friend's fathers even checked in to see how things were going. The Elliott Road Soap Box Derby was becoming a neighborhood event.

As time passed, our cars were beginning to really shape up. Each vehicle was well built, had its own paint job, a name on the hood and looked like a winner. The car Adam and I raced was painted yellow and named the Yellow Jacket. Reuben and Spencer's vehicle was black and designated The Black Beauty. Duane and Jimmy's racer was painted fire engine red and sported the label of the Red Rocket on her hood. The last car in our contest was going to be raced by Heath and Matt who called their beige racer the Brown Bullet. Each of these push cars looked great and we all were looking forward to racing one another in the First Elliott Road Push Car Derby.

We were putting the finishing touches on our cars one Friday evening when my grandfather began to question the location of our neighborhood race. He asked me how we were going to race all four of our cars on the narrow non-maintained access way behind our pasture. My grampa was worried and felt using the road my friends and I selected for our race was unsafe.

Early the following morning, I saw my grampa behind our pasture looking over the old road we had selected for our race. He paced the length of the old access way and appeared to be inspecting our proposed racing site thoroughly. When my grandfather came to breakfast, I asked what he had been doing. He told me he had measured the length as well as the width of our proposed race track and that he had studied the depth of the numerous pot holes dotting its surface as well.

He said his roadside survey confirmed his earlier suspicions that the old access way was totally unsuitable for our push car race because of its hazardous condition. He also declared he had another site in mind for our derby that was much more appropriate for our needs. He then surprised me when he said that with our help, he would fence off a section of our pasture and construct a flat and smooth racing oval better suited to our purpose.

Once again I was overjoyed by my grampa's news and I couldn't wait to tell my friends. Later that morning we each agreed to help build our new course and rushed to meet my grandfather who was already toiling on the Elliott Road race track. First, we moved the fence back far enough to allow adequate space for our derby course and the space for one of my

grandmother's old garden benches to accommodate the massive crowds of spectators we anticipated. Next, my grandfather took his tractor and went to work. He disked, as well as harrowed the ground, then planed it and finally rolled it to compact the soil he selected for our race course. The track he created was in the shape of a flat oval approximately fifty feet long and twenty-five feet wide. After my grandfather finished the track, I chalked the start/finish line and outlined the curves while my friends applied the finishing touches to our homemade push car venue.

We were finished before dinner and our race track was perfect.

Everybody was excited and we couldn't wait to get the races started the next day.

As we sat and admired our racing oval my grandfather announced, "We had better get home and cleaned up because we're going to have a barbecue for everyone who worked on the race track." Our pasture was instantly vacated and in no time the freshly washed track workers returned, accompanied by their wives and mothers. The ladies of the neighborhood helped my gramma prepared one of her feasts while grampa and I cooked the burgers. Everything tasted great and when everybody had eaten their fill my grampa called the racers and their fathers aside to discuss how we would conduct our version of the Soap Box Derby.

My grandfather had heard of the plans my friends and I had conjured for our version of the race.

He liked most of our ideas and recommended we slightly alter our racing program to include preliminary heats, mixing teams and switching cars to assure fairness. The heats were conducted in a clockwise direction and judges were placed for safety and fair play.

My grampa said, "This new format will give everyone more of a chance of winning."

The heats would consist of races of two cars at a time in two lap contests with the driver and pusher of each vehicle exchanging positions at the end of the first lap. We then would determine the preliminary race winner via the process of elimination to the one car that remained undefeated or secured the most victories. Once this progression was completed, everyone would take a break then we would divide our eight race car driver/pushers into new teams and cars to begin our racing competitions anew.

The overall winner's determination began with a series of races between the four combinations of contestants who collected the most preliminary race victories. The Elliott Road Push Car Victory Trophy would then be presented to the racing team that emerged victorious from that last, conclusive event of the day.

Before the races began, my grandfather loosely appointed the officials for the race. He then positioned the neighborhood fathers as turn judges, starters and officials, who in turn looked for fouls and disqualified any push car team that raced unsafely or cheated. My grandfather then appointed Adam's father as the official starter. To make things extra official, my friend's dad produced his old Teddy Roosevelt horse pistol as a starting gun. Grampa then set up a makeshift judge's stand in the center of the infield of the track and displayed a homemade checkered flag to wave at the winner of each race. My Grandfather also made sure the competitors could view the trophy they were vying for by perching that aged and rusted loving cup majestically on a nearby pile of hay bales. My Grampa concluded his duties by selecting the first two contestants of the race by drawing straws.

We had great fun as we raced our homebuilt push cars on that warm Sunday afternoon in late June. I recall one race I had with Adam as my partner against Reuben and Spencer.

The derby had just begun and our car, the Yellow Jacket, was pitted against their racer, The Black Beauty. We knew this race was going to be interesting and that we probably didn't stand a chance of beating the black team when powerful Reuben was pushing diminutive Spencer. Yet, Adam and I felt we had a distinct advantage over the Black Beauty team after our foes positions were rotated and the undersized Spencer was pushing oversized Reuben.

Both teams lined up for our contest with Reuben pushing Spencer in their jet black special versus Adam pushing me in our yellow racer. Each team was alert and ready when the booming rapport of that old .38 pistol signaled the start of the race. Immediately, The Black Beauty took the lead, while Adam struggled to keep up with Reuben's pace and I steered the Yellow Jacket. We found ourselves a distant three car lengths behind our rival's vehicle when they reached the mid-point of the race and shifted positions. We were upon our opponents in an instant, I hit the brakes hard to stop, then Adam and I quickly rotated places and we were off in pursuit of our black foe. Suddenly, my team's fortunes dramatically changed for the better on the second lap of our contest. The Black Beauty had significantly slowed down with little Spencer now pushing the enormous weight of his colossal counterpart. On the contrary, I had no trouble pushing my evenly sized teammate past our challenger's car and we raced The Yellow Jacket on to victory.

Our win over Reuben and Spencer inspired my recollection of the tale of "The Tortoise and the Hare."

I promptly shared my thoughts with Adam. My reserved friend smiled then calmly stated. "We were just lucky and had better move out of the way." I agreed and we both pushed The Yellow Jacket off the track to make way for the next race.

After we parked our car, Adam and I shook hands with Reuben and Spencer to show no hard feelings. We then decided to take a break, sit down to sip some lemonade and share our exploits from the recent race. After we refreshed ourselves, we changed partners and cars then continued to race against one another throughout that memorable afternoon. Everyone won at least one race, nobody got hurt and we felt our version of push car racing was as good as any Soap Box Derby ever held.

Racing push cars in my grampa's pasture was great fun. I am yet amazed as to how the dream my friends and I had of racing Soap Box Derby cars turned into such a positive enterprise with the full involvement of my friends and their families. The brightly painted homemade cars and that wonderful track my grandfather constructed remain brilliant in my memory. I'll never forget how fantastic it was to see the joy on my grandfather's face as he watched everyone take pleasure in the neighborhood event we dubbed the Elliott Road Soap Box Derby.

Chapter 14

Bronco Busting

Attempting to ride wild horses was probably the most amusing and rowdy episode Adam, Duane, Spencer and I ever had as boys. The small horses we chose as our mounts were mature, undomesticated and rescued by Mr. Milligan, who had a horse farm not far from my grandfather's house. Mr. Milligan loved his horses and we knew we would have to ask him politely if we were to have any chance of riding his six little chargers.

One sunny spring morning the four of us summoned courage and approached the squire of the horse farm down the road. We came to the grand gate of the Bar M Ranch and warily entered the premises. Immediately we saw Mr. Milligan riding his white horse in a distant pasture.

He quickly caught sight of us and we stood frozen on the dusty road leading to his grand mansion as he approached.

He was at our side in an instant and wanted to know if anything was wrong. We shook our heads and I asked him if it would be alright if we could ride his little ponies. Mr. Milligan laughed and said, "Go ahead, but be careful."

He then cautioned us and said that those little ponies weren't really ponies and that they weren't accustomed to being ridden. He told us they were fully grown, downsized, mining horses he had recently saved from extermination on public land in Oregon's high desert. He also told us there were ropes in the horse barn   we could use for harnesses, but no saddles, and we were to be sure to keep the corral gate closed. We eagerly agreed and thanked the gentleman, who then majestically rode away on his noble steed.

We ran to the barn to get our makeshift tack, then cautiously made our way to the corral and entered the gate.

The horses weren't scared by our bold entry and stood calmly looking at the four invaders of their paddock. Spencer and Duane immediately climbed to the top rail of the corral fence to watch Adam and I present our version of horsemanship.

I was amazed at how docile the ponies were as we cautiously approached them. The little horses just stood still and calmly allowed both Adam and I to pet and dress them with our makeshift hackamores. I thought to myself "This isn't going to be any fun because these mounts have no spirit."

Things instantly changed when we attempted to ride Mr. Milligan's quiet little horses. Those docile animals turned into fireballs that bucked and jumped with all their might the moment anybody attempted to ride them. They behaved like the wild bucking broncos we had seen in the cowboy movies and we each had an absolute blast getting thrown all over the corral by the little mounts.

Those tiny horses acted in a most curious manner following our encounters. Once they rid themselves of our pesky equitational attempts, the minute chargers immediately returned to their passive demeanors.

The tough little horses would come to us and nudge us to our feet for another ride immediately after violently bucking us from their backs. This sudden change in equine behavior was puzzling to say the least. I had never witnessed such a dramatic behavioral transition in an animal. Those ponies continually changed their moods from passive to violent and back to passive. One thing was for sure, those diminutive horses didn't want to be ridden and anybody who attempted to mount them could count on an unceremonious trip to the ground.

The four of us didn't care if we ever rode those ponies – we just had fun playing with them while getting thrown from their backs.

My approach was always the same. I would calmly and softly draw near my quarry, then pet and softly speak to my equine candidate as I carefully slipped the rope around its neck. Once these preliminaries were finished and I felt satisfied with my selected steed's disposition, I would jump on as fast as I could. The similitude of my approach was equal to the sameness of its result. I was immediately bucked off, then nudged and comforted by the pony I was trying to ride as I sat sulking in the dirt.

We had some terrible spills, but we didn't get hurt since our safety was insured by two factors. Our well being was first gauranteed by the short stance of the horses themselves which in turn equated to a lesser distance to the ground after we were ejected from our mounted positions. The second factor which contributed to our protection was the soft condition of the ground. The spongy consistency of the turf around the corral was due to recent rains and a welcome benefit from Mother Nature. Nevertheless, the size of the horses and the condition of the corral turf didn't diminish the fun we had with those diminutive broncos.

I recall one wild ride I had on a little mare I informally named Sally. After getting the rope around her neck, I jumped to her back and she took off. For a second, I thought I was going to ride her, but she bolted, then got me riding on her rump and the next thing I knew, I was flying over the coral fence.

Adam had a fantastic fall also. He mounted his micro steed, we informally dubbed Tornado, only to witness his horse jump in a backward motion, landing my friend on the little stallion's neck as it backed out from under his weight eventually landing our would-be cowboy in the water trough.

Duane had a rough fall attempting to ride a mount we called Lollipop. Duane decided to change his approach from the method Adam and I were utilizing. He made the decision to approach his charger Indian style from the rear with a running start, then leapfrog onto the horse's back before the animal knew what happened. He decided to not use a harness, instead utilizing the pony's mane as his method of control. Duane began his Native American attempt at horsemanship by slowly entering the corral and carefully selecting Lollipop as his horse of opportunity.

He positioned himself several feet behind the little mare then ran and jumped to ride her.

Characteristically, Lollipop saw Duane coming and bolted at the last second, leaving my friend clinging to the horse's rump, half on and half off. Duane was then involuntarily paraded around the paddock, concluding his humiliating attempt by being bucked headlong into a fresh pile of manure.

Spencer also had a memorable tumble from one of the Milligan Ranch mining horses. Spencer was too small to mount those broncos himself so he ingeniously overcame his disability by climbing the corral fence and then jumping onto the back of the horse he selected to ride from his newfound elevation. After a few attempts, Spencer had become fairly skilled at this improvisation. His bucking episode began with his copious selection of a small steed as a target. Next, Spenser deftly stalked his quarry to a suitable position where he could climb the corral fence and jump on the little horses back. As soon as my friend lit on the little charger the horse immediately spun around and flicked Spenser into the center of the coral. Our would-be cowboy landed flat on his back and the blow from the fall temporarily knocked the air out of him. We all ran to Spencer's assistance and quickly got our little friend to his feet as his mount, who we later dubbed Spinner, softly nudged him as if to say, "no hard feelings."

After several hours, Mr. Milligan came by to see how we were doing. He saw the four of us having the time of our lives.

Our benefactor was laughing as hard as we were.

He said, "How about some lemonade." We had worked up quite a thirst in that corral and jumped at the chance for some refreshment. We earnestly followed Mr. Milligan to the house where his wife had prepared some of her refreshing lemonade.

My friends and I eagerly told the friendly couple of the fun we had experienced getting knocked all over the corral by those fantastic little horses. Mr. and Mrs. Milligan were very nice to us and we wanted to repay them for the fun we had on their ranch. I asked Mr. Milligan if there was anything we could do to help him with his horses. Mr. Milligan asked if we knew anything about horses.

I told him I had an old horse named Smokey that I fed and watered daily. Mr. Milligan was glad and announced he would take us to the corral and show us how to care for his livestock.

When we got to the corral, our squire led us to the barn and gave us brushes to groom our new equine friends.

We devotedly brushed, fed then watered the little horses and Mr. Milligan was pleased with our sincere interest. Those miniature mounts were great, they allowed Spencer, Adam, Duane and I to handle and groom them without incident. Mr. Milligan told us we were becoming good horsemen and said we could come back and ride his little horses whenever we felt like it.

We often went to the Bar M ranch to attempt to ride Mr. Milligan's mini-horses. We were never successful as bronco busters, but it sure was fun trying to ride those puzzling and playful animals as we grew in the beautiful pastoral environment of the Rogue River Valley.

Chapter 15

Archery and Games of Robin Hood

My friends and I were introduced to the story of Robin Hood and the sport of archery simultaneously in the spring of my fifth grade year. Our school featured the classic old English tale as part of the Literary curriculum and the sport of archery was introduced to us as part of the Howard Elementary Physical Education program. The two courses complimented one another from an educational standpoint and my friends and I were eager to learn all we could of both topics.

The tale of Robin Hood was presented to us for study by Mr. Bailey, our home room teacher. Robin Hood and his merry men was ideal subject matter to be read and enjoyed by my neighborhood group of pre-adolescent boys. The knights in armor, the archery and the garish adventure enthralled my friends and I, while the pastoral setting of Robin Hood was very similar to the bucolic surroundings we grew up in.

159

As we studied the classic legend, my friends and I began to imagine ourselves involved in some heroic scenario at our hero's side, defending the poor from the rich.

In no time, our troop was completely engrossed by the timeless narrative and we each assumed the roles of our favorite characters.

Archery class was conducted as part of the regular physical education program of Howard Elementary. Coach Collie was our instructor and regulated our archery activities scrupulously. The equipment was suited to our age level with light weight bows and target tipped arrows. Our objectives consisted of hay bales fitted with targets and stationed at ten then finally 20 yard intervals.

Coach Collie stressed safety at all times and we became well versed in the careful handling of this new and different type of weapon. Our mentor taught us how to safely check and use our equipment. Mr. Collie also trained us how to string and unstring a bow in addition to giving us the skills necessary for aiming and shooting our arrows. With practice under the patient guidance of Coach Collie, my friends and I became fairly skilled at archery. Each of us progressed in ability to hit the bull's eye of a target at a distance of ten yards with a fair amount of regularity.

Mr. Bailey grew increasingly impressed with the interest and knowledge we retained from reading about our old English hero as well as our avid participation in archery. Ultimately, Mr. Bailey worked with Coach Collie to allow our class extra time to study our hero and practice archery concurrently via a unique series of lesson plans specifically designed to coordinate the two disciplines. The extra periods of study were a magnificent experience for me and my band of merry men. Those lesson plans gave each of us a unique perspective in learning while we both physically and mentally explored the nexus of archery as it applied to the classic English narrative. Consequently, the learning experience designed by Mr. Bailey and Coach Collie gave each of us a significantly higher level of understanding of both Robin Hood and the sport of archery.

One day in early June, Coach Collie called my friends and I aside and told us, "You are all showing a lot of promise as archers. You can purchase your own archery equipment locally."

He then made available the literature containing all the specifics we would need for the equipment suitable to our ages and purpose. My friends and I riotously responded to Mr. Collie's presentation then took his notes to our parents for final approval. Our parents consented to our petition. Then, after saving the money we gleaned from our allowances plus extra chores we rushed to the Big Y to purchase our own bows, arrows and quivers.

By the time school closed for the year, we were ready for an adventurous summer reliving the story of our ancient English hero and testing our newly acquired archery skills. We played games of Robin Hood and simulated the roles of the key figures of the account whenever we could. It was great fun and our mothers joined in the amusement by making us rudimentary costumes to enhance our fantasies. We wore our costumes throughout the summer as we sought adventure in our bucolic environment masquerading as the characters from our favorite boyhood tale.

The Grand Archery Tournament was an event my merry men and I played in our pasture when Romeo was away performing acts of husbandry and Smokey was safely corralled.

We replicated the account from the Old English narrative as best we could and used a hay bale as a makeshift target.

The grand prize of a golden arrow was hewn from a discarded curtain rod and seemed curiously suitable to our needs.

The rules of our archery tournament were simple and few. Each archer was allowed to shoot a maximum of ten arrows towards the mark of a large red dot painted on our selected cube of straw preset to a distance of twenty paces. Pincer movements, barrages and frontal assaults were each undertaken in those make-believe attacks. Once an archer had exhausted his supply of arrows, all the competitors went to the target to assess his score. Scores were calculated under the following formula: 10 points was awarded for a bull's eye and one point was given for scoring a hit on the target itself. The scores of our grand archery tournament were relatively low with the score of fifty points earning Duane (King Arthur) the coveted arrow of brass.

Storming the castle was another Robin Hood game we staged in our pasture when it was vacated of livestock. The citadel was actually a large neat pile of hay bales my grandfather erected to serve as Smokey and Romeo's winter feed. My friends and I regarded that haystack as the adversarial Nottingham Castle and continually sought to fill that imaginary fortress with the projectiles launched from our bows.

My friends and I concocted an infinite number of scenarios and strategies to storm that imaginary fortification. Our fictitious castle was manned with fanciful cardboard

guards who stood no chance against our band of valorous merry men. It was great fun inventing ourselves as the various characters of the Old English tale while we stormed the walls of that imaginary citadel and those ramparts of silage fell under the onslaught of our arrows.

Shooting our arrows while bike riding, (no hands) was another game my friends and I took pleasure in as we imagined ourselves the characters from the Robin Hood legend.

This game also utilized our recently acquired archery skills as well as my grandparent's pasture, when Romeo and Smokey were safely absent from the mayhem. We dubbed this game Arrows on the Fly and utilized our bikes instead of the mighty steeds of the English classic.

To play Arrows on the Fly, we first placed discarded melons atop strategically aligned fence posts that bordered my grandparent's vacated pasture. We then decorated the posts to look like the evil King John's men. Next, we would race our bikes past our imaginary adversaries while we shot as many arrows as we could toward the hapless melons. Our band of merry men loved to play Arrows on the Fly, and we soon became fairly skilled at shooting arrows into those spoiled gourds from the seat of our speeding bikes.

As time passed, my merry men and I tired of Arrows on the Fly and our vivid boyhood imaginations concocted other improvisational Robin Hood oriented activities to appreciate.

One bright summer day after chores, my band of heroes and I were discussing the potential for adventure in the woods near my house. Duane, who was of Native American heritage, told us of a game his ancestors played as children. We dubbed this ancient game Tree to Tree, and then transformed it into one of our Robin Hood styled amusements.

To play Tree to Tree, my friends and I first reconnoitered a section of the woods that bordered the Rouge River next to Touville Park and a short bikeride from my house. We surveyed the geography of our game site with disregard for problems associated with the thick brush in search of large trees to mark as targets for our arrows. After several trees were selected we put together a course to follow.

We then would take turns individually racing on foot through our forested course to see who could shoot the most arrows into the most targeted trees in the shortest amount of time.

Hawkeye usually won the contests of Tree to Tree due to his exceptional skill in aiming and shooting arrows as well as his uncanny ability to navigate through the thick wooded undergrowth. We each loved that game and neither poison oak, mosquito bites, ticks, bruises nor cuts or scratches could ever dissuade our hearty group from playing Tree to Tree.

The adventures my friends and I had while playing Robin Hood were wonderful as well as educational. Those escapades allowed me and my merry men to act out and learn the tales portrayed in that Old English storybook while we educated ourselves and became proficient in archery. I will always remember with fondness the games of Robin Hood we played during those golden summer days of my boyhood.

Chapter 16

The Elliott Road Zeppelin Works

Building and flying a model Zeppelin was another aeronautical adventure I had with Harry, Adam and Jimmy.

This kit was exclusively designed and planned by our elder modeler, Harry, and after re-design and modification, it really flew. Our lighter than air replica was constructed from cardboard and imitated a real airship in rough detail. However, our Zeppelin simulated the original giants of the air with one explicit aspect. It utilized hydrogen as a primary means of rising aloft.

Our model Zeppelin was a replica of the Hindenburg, a German lighter than air ship that tragically crashed and burned after a transatlantic crossing in Lakehurst, New Jersey, on May 5, 1937. We designed our first version of the Hindenburg to include beautiful detail for every inch of her eight foot length and one foot 6 inch diameter. Harry had spent a great deal of time reading about the Zeppelins flown by the Germans in the early part of the twentieth century. He had acquired a great deal of knowledge concerning the construction, design and flight of these lighter than air ships. Harry felt confident he could design then direct Adam, Jimmy and I to assist in the construction of a flying scale model of the Hindenburg.

There were several immediate problems that had to be addressed if our lighter than airship was to fly. The first problem we had to overcome was how to create hydrogen. The second problem we faced was how to securely and safely house this volatile gas within the structural confines of the model. Other problems consisted of weight to lift parameters, safe propulsion via the utilization of internal combustion engines, the selection of materials that were strong and light enough to complete the task at hand as well as devising a means to safely control the airship in flight.

The issues of creating the hydrogen for our project and housing the highly flammable material was solved by Harry who learned he could produce this gas by placing aluminum foil in a mixture of lye and water. He next devised a plan to safely deliver, capture and utilize, our homemade hydrogen by partially filling a discarded pop bottle with the material's prime ingredients then capping his make shift gas chamber with a balloon. After the escaping gas had sufficiently filled the inflatable balloon, Harry tied it off and a buoyant, flexible bag of lighter than air material was created. Our leader then stated it was just a matter of constructing compartments within the framework of our Zeppelin to house the bags of hydrogen created via his ingenious pop bottle method.

The next problem Harry tackled was how big to make our model as opposed to how much gas it would take to lift our Hindenburg skyward. Our leader had studied several books on the subject and decided it would take six hydrogen filled balloons evenly placed within the framework of our Zeppelin to lift a model that was eight feet long by one foot six inches in diameter. For safety, Harry decided on a plan to enclose the hydrogen balloons within cardboard compartments equipped with removable bottom covers. As an extra margin of safety, we would cover the entire ship in tissue painted with flame retardant paint.

The propulsion for our Hindenburg was to be provided for by six .020 internal combustion engines. Harry designed these little dynamos to be housed on evenly spaced pods fastened to the sides of the ship. We each felt this engine placement was a good idea to suit the scale appearance of the kit and to accommodate the safety requirements of the model.

The framing for our lighter than air ship was substantial. The structure included; the main rings as well as bracing necessary for the enclosed compartments to house the hydrogen filled balloons, the six .020 gas motor pods, a small compartment to house the lead split shot necessary to maintain slightly positive buoyancy and a highly detailed gondola. These requirements demanded a lot of balsa wood be utilized with constant attention being paid to the weight of the model.

The final problem Harry addressed in his plans was the design of flight controls for our Zeppelin. First, Harry felt elevator control was not necessary as the hydrogen would take care of lift. Directional management was accounted for by fitting the rudder of our model with a fifteen degree offset. This offset would insure our model would be directed in a circle and assist in the control of our Zeppelin. Finally, a one hundred foot piece of fishing line was to be securely attached to the gondola of our airship as a tether to provide additional insurance in avoiding fly aways.

After briefing us on the plans for our Zeppelin, Harry gave Adam, Jimmy and I our construction assignments. Adam and Harry would work on the gondola and exterior motor pods while Dennis and I worked on the framing. Then we all would apply the tissue and painting applications to our version of the Hindenburg.

Framing this model was a daunting task. Work progressed slowly at first until Jimmy and I figured out how to frame all the struts and bulkheads of our airship in a light and strong manner according to Harry's master plan.

We finally figured things out and after many hours of labor we presented our completed framework to our mentor for final inspection and testing.

Strength, weight and trueness of shape were the preeminent factors Harry wanted built into the framing of our Hindenburg. Every part had to be evaluated for weight and structural integrity. Harry wanted our kit's skeleton to be light and strong as well as faithful to the uniform contour of the original Zeppelin. Our mentor first examined the overall construction of our airship's framing. Our chief designer noted the framing was true and square with the bulkheads and other vital compartments placed securely and balanced within our Zeppelin's structure. Next, Harry carefully weighed the balsa framework of our kit.

He said it was going to be close and everybody began to worry.

We took the skeleton of our model Hindenburg to my grandfather's cool moist pasture. Our leader set up his makeshift gas chamber and began to create hydrogen immediately after we arrived at our flying field.

Next, Harry filled the six balloons he had selected for our model with the volatile gas. He then placed the balloons in the compartments Jimmy and I constructed within our kits fuselage. Everything was set and tensions were high. Our leader looked to Jimmy and me then released our Zeppelin to see if it would float in the air.

Our first test was a failure. Our Zeppelin sank to the ground like a balsa stone, never to be released from our planet's firm gravitational hold. We each looked at one another in shock then began to re-think how to correct this embarrassing oversight.

Harry began re-evaluating our airship by testing the efficacy of our hydrogen gas and reviewing the structural notes he had of the earlier German Zeppelins. The next morning we again went to the pasture and Harry tested the flammability and lift of the hydrogen he created. First, he filled a large balloon with the volatile gas, attached a homemade fuse to the base of the inflatable, lit the fuse and released it into the sky.

The balloon quickly rose aloft and in a few seconds blew up in a flash of white light then quickly disintegrated. Harry said the test of our hydrogen was a success due to the brightness of the flash and the complete disintegration of the balloon.

We then examined the lifting value of our gas by filling balloons with the volatile material and checking the lifting value of each balloon with a pre-weighted load of balsa wood equal to one sixth of the total weight of the framing. We soon found the individual balloons could not lift their sectional loads.

We then resolved to drastically alter the construction plans for our model to assure the success of our airship.

After much adjustment and re-configuring, a new design for our model Hindenburg was created. These new plans altered a lot of the features Harry had previously wanted and deleted much of the framing he formerly insisted on. The result was a much lighter and a less scaled replica of that grand German airship.

Basically, our new version of the Hindenburg was equal in size to our first model. However, our newest Zeppelin differed greatly from our original in construction and was built solely from a series of thin, lightweight cardboard slats copiously taped together.

Fins were attached to the rear of our model for appearance and a gaping ventral cavity was established from its nose to tail in order to house six loosely placed gas filled balloons. The motor pods and engines were discarded for weight considerations and controls were deleted with the exception of four pieces of fishing line, used as tow lines, and attached to the nose, tail and sides of our model respectively. Painting was not necessary as the back of the cardboard we utilized was factory painted a shade of gray that replicated the paint scheme of the original Airship.

Our cardboard Zeppelin was finished in a little more than a week and the four of us were excited to see her fly.

Early the next day, we marched our model to my grampa's pasture as visions of the Hindenburg crash filled our minds.

We arrived at our flying field quickly and the smell of moist alfalfa reminded us of the margin of safety that green silage provided against the instability of the gas soon to be housed in our model's fuselage. Harry began the launch of our model by filling six balloons with the hydrogen he made and carefully positioned the inflatables in the airship.

Immediately, we could see this version of Germany's grand Zeppelin was going to be a success. Our cardboard model rose and floated on the air like a cloud. Harry held her securely by the lead line then assigned Adam, Jimmy and me one of the remaining three tow lines. I marveled at our replicated Zeppelin as the four of us triumphantly walked our model around the field behind my house.

Constructing a working model of a Zeppelin was the most challenging, educational and unforgettable undertaking of my modeling career. I will forever recall the hours Jimmy and I spent painstakingly crafting the balsa framework of our failed replica of the Hindenburg. I also recall Harry's experiments with hydrogen and learning of the volatility of that gas.

This endeavor was also etched in my mind as a despondent milestone of my life. My sorrow began immediately following the maiden flight of our airship when Harry announced he wasn't going to be available to assist us with our models any longer. Our lead modeler was leaving us to join the Air Force in a few short days and we knew we would never see him again.

Harry's departure was a harbinger of the future as each member of our group began to ponder what was to come.

174

Things were changing. Our world was getting bigger and each of us was evolving from children into young men with differing interests and capabilities.

My friends and I began to comprehend that Medford, too, was beginning to be transformed from a quiet rural haven to a bustling center of commerce. The quiet countryside and pastoral beauty of our area was soon to be distorted into a suburban setting of houses, strip malls and traffic.

Our golden days of summer were soon to be a memory as each member of our group grew and followed separate paths.

Chapter 17

Folkways

The wonderful and formative experiences
I had as a growing Oregonian boy included
encounters with a variety of people embracing a
wide range of deep-rooted customs and traditions.
I have chosen to label those practices folkways. To me,
these folkways were genuine in their believed purpose.
To others, they had no merit whatsoever and were often
shunned by the vast majority of our local populace or
even denounced as witchcraft. However, I found each of
these folkways historically interesting, socially dynamic
and illustrative of the Rogue River Valley's unique cultural
underpinnings.

There were several folkways I recall that covered a wide
variety of topics. Religious snake handling, Holy Rolling,

rainmaking, vining, planting by the moon, moon shining and folk medicine are a few of the traditional folk customs I remember most.

Religious snake handling or religious serpent handling has a curious and lengthy history. This ritual has been practiced by a small number of churches for approximately one hundred years. Religious serpent handling was begun in Appalachia and has expanded as a movement of worship over the past several decades.

Religious snake handling was a folkway I came across indirectly while on a fishing trip to the Applegate River.

It was early on Saturday one warm summer morning when my friends Adam and Duane joined me for a trip to one of our favorite fishing spots. This was one of the few times Duane was able to escape having to chaperone his little brother and we were all glad for the respite away from Spencer.

My friends arrived at my house before dawn and impatiently lingered while I quickly loaded my bike with the necessary equipment. The sun was beginning to rise when the three of us eagerly headed for our angling destination some twenty miles distant on our favorite waterway.

This was our first fishing trip of the year and we had pedaled several miles when we suddenly came upon a mysterious structure. There, back in the trees some five hundred feet from the road, was a familiar old farmhouse covered in a new paint scheme and freshly decorated with a large cross. We stopped and glanced at the property, and then Adam loudly exclaimed, "Wow there must be a new church in town."

The three of us looked to one another with curious eagerness, then Duane said, "Let's scout this out."

My friends and I rode cautiously down the long wooded driveway to investigate. Adam's guess was confirmed when we reached the end of the approach. The old farmhouse had indeed been transformed into a church with clean landscaping and a new coat of lustrous white paint.

Duane and I decided to explore the entire exterior of the building while Adam peeked through the windows of this newly remodeled edifice.

After we regrouped Adam said, "It's got a church look!"

Duane and I then stared through the window and saw pews, a pulpit, a large crucifix behind an altar plus several other curious items Adam had over looked. There, in the rear of the church were several glass containers that resembled empty aquariums each housing a large rattlesnake.

We stepped back from the window and again looked to one another in bewilderment then immediately decided to conclude our sojourn and report the disturbing white structure to our parents.

We completely forgot about our fishing trip and couldn't wait to get back to the familiar surroundings of our neighborhood. I saw my grandfather working in the pasture as I raced into the carport to park my bike. I jumped from my ride and then dashed to tell him of the weird experience my friends and I had just witnessed.

I was so excited I could hardly speak and eventually managed to communicate my troubling encounter.

My grandfather could see I was upset and in a benevolent tone said, "Come along and we'll sort this out in the kitchen."

As soon as we entered the house my grandmother knew something was amiss. My grandfather told her of my adventure and she motioned for my grandfather and me to sit down at the table. My gramma quickly fetched a supply of milk and cookies, then sat down with us to discuss my disconcerting escapade.

I began my explanation with a lengthy and dramatic description of the strange experience I had earlier that morning. I anxiously illustrated the shiny white house furnished like a church and the numerous odd containers that accommodated venomous serpents in the back of the main hall behind the pews. My grandparents could see I was upset and calmed my frayed nerves with a logical explanation.

My grandmother began to explain to me how different people worshiped the Lord in different ways.

She said, "Serpent worship is a way some folks believed to praise the Lord." My Gramma went on to tell me, "Don't be afraid. People in America are free to worship the Lord as they see fit."

My grandfather then kindly but firmly told me, "Stay away from that place and don't bother those people."

My grandparent's words soothed me and, as the days passed, I began to ponder how curious some cultural beliefs and traditions were. Slowly, I overcame my initial shock from exposure to religious snake handling and accepted this historically pious practice as a fascinating example of the contributory folkways appurtenant to the rural environment of my childhood.

Holy Rolling was another long-established religious custom I inadvertently encountered in the rustic surroundings of my youth. The term, Holy Roller, is generally regarded negatively as a label for the demonstrative method of worship adopted by some Christians.

This emotional devotion includes the believer rolling on the floor or speaking in tongues after he or she is completely enveloped by the Lord's grace.

The history associated with this religious practice in America is also long and like serpent handling spans a period of over one hundred years. The extensive period of time associated with Holy Rolling testifies to the spiritual popularity of this religious practice and clearly establishes this method of worship as a folkway.

The summer of my twelfth year was particularly hot. Accordingly, my friends and I took many trips to our local swimming pool in search of relief. Those treks led us past a new and curious building being constructed on the edge of town. This edifice had been catching interest in our hamlet since ground was broken for its construction early the preceding spring. No signs were ever erected and nobody was ever available to state the purpose of the ambiguous structure.

My exposure to Holy Rolling commenced one hot Sunday afternoon when Adam, Duane, Spencer and I grouped at my house before journeying to our town's Aquatic Park. After everyone was set, we mounted our bikes and began the expedition to our shady oasis with all speed. It wasn't long before we came upon the mysterious structure that had captivated everyone's imagination over the past several months. We noted that the construction was completed and a large Christian cross had been added to the standard architecture.

The building was landscaped in a pleasant and recognizable manner. We realized our mystery structure was a church with a parking lot full of cars owned by the large congregation attending worship inside.

As we rode closer to this mysterious house of worship, we soon realized something was amiss. We could hear loud screaming and singing and saw the doors and windows were left wide open. Our boyhood curiosities were fully aroused as we parked our bikes and crept closer to the front door of the edifice. We were astonished when we peeked in and saw the church packed with finely clothed people rolling around on the floor screaming and singing praises of the lord as loudly as humanly possible.

Immediately, we ran back to our bikes and looked to one another, jaws agape in amazement .What had we seen? Were we sure of what we had seen? Were we in the Twilight Zone? This spectacle was very odd and something we had only heard of in the ribald yarns my grandfather spun.

Suddenly, Duane yelled, "They're Holy Rollers," whereupon we immediately mounted our bikes and headed home to explain the horrors we had seen.

We pedaled as fast as we could to the sanctity of my yard, then everyone ran into my grandmother's house to tell her what we had witnessed and ask if we should call the police or maybe the National Guard. As usual my grandmother calmly evaluated our state of shock, sat us down and served us lemonade and cookies. She then undertook the task of explaining what we had previously observed on the edge of town.

My gramma said, "Those people were Christians and though different, were just celebrating the Lord in their own harmless way."

My grandmother's explanation soothed our shaken, youthful state of mind and all was well. We continued to eat our snacks as we talked over our ordeal. After a short while, we each felt comfortable enough to continue with our affairs of the day.

Ultimately, we decided to renew our ride to Hawthorne Pool and avoid the summer heat secure in the knowledge of our town's newest church, though different, was harmless and was not to be feared.

As time passed I realized the Christians I encountered on that summer afternoon were practicing another time honored rural custom. I came to appreciate this interesting folkway for its unique cultural content and something vital to the social definition of my rural surroundings.

Rainmaking was another folkway I encountered as a boy growing up in rural southern Oregon. The History of rainmaking in America can be traced back to the Great Plains during the latter half of the 19th century. This curious folkway gained immense popularity in the Midwest during the Dust Bowl Days of the 1930's and as the years passed, the practice of artificially attempting to producing rain made its way to Oregon and the Rogue Valley.

I was introduced to rainmaking via a neighbor of my grandparents, Don Baker. Mr. Baker was an interesting old man. Everybody jokingly knew him as Baker, the Rain Maker. He lived down the road from my grandparent's house in a rundown dwelling that always featured an odd assortment of strange, brightly colored equipment on display in his front yard.

One summer morning, I passed Mr. Baker's house on my way to the Big Y and saw him tinkering with some of his peculiar equipment. The disheveled condition of the rainmaker's house as well as his eerie equipment aroused my suspicion. Ultimately, my thirteen year old curiosity overcame my fear and I decided to find out everything I could about this anomalous man and his curious cultural tradition.

Cautiously, I got off my bike then approached the old would be weather man. My odd neighbor looked up from his labors and said, "I'm Baker the Rain Maker, what do you need."

Mr. Baker was tall, bearded and clothed in old, soiled overalls, worn boots and a tattered straw hat. His overture amused me and I smiled, then the two of us began to laugh. I found Mr. Baker friendly and easy to talk to as my former feelings of distrust vanished. I began a dialogue with this enigmatic country rascal and pestered him with ten thousand boyish questions in my attempt to gain knowledge of rainmaking. Baker, the Rainmaker patiently answered all of my queries as he showed me every piece of his equipment and its associated use.

I was surprised at the volume of his comprehension of this mysterious subject and began to appreciate the folkway he embraced.

It was well past noon when Mr. Baker concluded his talk.

He then looked into the sky and said, "Come on by tomorrow and I'll show you how to make rain." I eagerly agreed and my mind began to fill with dramatic images of cloudbursts and torrential rainfall.

I pedaled over to Adam's house after my call on Baker the Rainmaker. I excitedly told my friend of my meteorological adventure and found him less than impressed. Adam didn't believe in rainmaking and felt anybody who claimed to make rain was full of beans. I vehemently disagreed and the two of us began to argue. I informed Adam about Mr. Baker's brightly colored equipment and how each device worked in a harmonious, scientific manner to create rainfall. Adam was not swayed and the more I talked the less he was convinced.

Finally I realized I was getting nowhere on the subject and challenged my friend to come with me to Mr. Baker's house the following day and see a real rainmaker in action. Adam laughingly agreed and everything was set, if my grandparents consented.

Suddenly, I realized it was getting late. I bid my pal a hasty goodbye then rode on to my house. I made it home in time to help my grandfather with the evening's barbecue.

I was loading the briquettes when the man I revered most asked me what I had been doing that day. I eagerly told him of my adventure with Baker the Rainmaker and jubilantly waited for his response. My grampa replied, "Rainmaking is a fake as well as a form of witchcraft and you are foolish to waste your time with such senselessness."

I was shocked by the response I received from my grandfather. I was sure rainmaking was a scientific means to change the weather and that Baker the Rainmaker was somebody to be revered instead of ridiculed.

My grandparents and I discussed rainmaking extensively during dinner. They repeatedly said that this questionable means of making a living was a form of witchcraft and explained why I shouldn't waste my time with such silliness. My gramma went on to say, "Anybody who attempts to make rain is crazy and subject to the whims of the devil." I tried to counter my grandparent's viewpoint with the contention that rainmaking was scientific, but to no avail.

Slowly, I worked up the courage to ask if I could go to Mr. Baker's house in the morning with Adam to see Mr. Baker make rain. I anxiously awaited my grandparent's reply and after several tense moments of silence, my grandfather shrugged his shoulders and my grandmother reluctantly told me I could go. I was euphoric and immediately telephoned Adam to tell him of the good news.

Adam arrived at my house after breakfast the next morning. My grandmother asked if we still intended to go through with our visit to Mr. Baker then handed each of us a lunch for the trip. She told us, "I will be praying for you."

She then asked us to be careful and my friend and I agreed. Adam and I concluded our parting conversation with my grandmother with a generous quantity of glib slogans and assurances of our safe return in the afternoon.

We arrived at Baker, the Rainmaker's house around 10 a.m. and saw him busily setting up his equipment in the field behind his house. There was a large brush pile, a carbide cannon, a drum, a brightly painted table, a big golden bowl filled with something labeled "Rain Spices," several sections of shiny aluminum pipe planted on end into the ground and a bucket of water soaking an old blanket. I turned to Adam with a scowl of affirmation, then introduced my skeptical friend to Baker, the Rainmaker.

The old weather wizard boisterously introduced himself to Adam, then began his rainmaking procedure. He started his ritual by igniting the brush pile, then uttering a mysterious chant as he pranced around the blaze tossing his rain spices on the embers. Next, he picked up his drum and began to strike a basic rhythm. After several minutes of drumming the rainmaker picked up the wet blanket then alternately covered and uncovered the fire to create smoke puffs. As the smoke lifted, he struck the grounded aluminum pipes with his drumstick and created an ominous deep tone.

He ended his first session in rainless failure with the loud rapport from his carbide cannon that he said, "Would wake the "gods".

The old meteorological magic man conducted several more rainmaking sessions that day, with each exercise ending unsuccessfully. I expectantly watched the old man put on his show repeatedly throughout the afternoon, but no rain ever fell and there wasn't a cloud to be seen in the blue sky above. Gradually, I realized my grandparents were right. Rainmaking was a fake and I had been fooled by Baker, the Rainmaker.

It was mid-afternoon when Adam and I left Mr. Baker's theatrical exhibition and headed home. At first, I felt ashamed for being duped into believing in rainmaking and I was grateful for the kind reassurances my friend gave me. I'll forever remember Adam's genuine and caring attitude that day and how he never seized the opportunity to verbally reinforce how wrong I was.

As time passed, I re-valuated rainmaking as a custom. Slowly I came to value rainmaking as a vital folkway valued by some who lived in our rural surrounding and an elemental component to the cultural composition of which I was a part.

Vining was one more folkway I became aware of as I grew up in southern Oregon. Some of my friends viewed

Vining as nonsense or another form of witchcraft. The Smith family were often ridiculed for practicing its techniques. Yet, this non-traditional method of locating underground water sources intrigued me and I was eager to learn all I could of this time-honored tradition.

Vining, also known as water witching or dowsing, possesses a long narration. America's historical association with dowsing can be recounted from the early settlers of the upper Midwest in the latter part of the nineteenth century. The pioneers who settled from the Dakotas through northern Ohio practiced dowsing on a regular basis as a means of locating water for their crops, their livestock and their general survival. As the years went by, vining moved westward with the settlement of the west and eventually made its way to the Rogue River Valley.

My exposure to vining came via Harry and Jimmy's dad, Mr. Smith. Mr. Smith was a farmer by profession and practiced vining as a productive means of locating water. He was well known as a dowser and people would pay my friend's father generous sums of money to find water on their respective properties.

As time passed, my friends could see I was genuinely interested in learning all I could about vining. Harry and Jimmy told me their family were of Bohemian descent and immigrated to the United States at the beginning of the twentieth century.

My friends also informed me many of their ancestors were well known Bohemian dowsers and this useful art was a valued family tradition passed from father to son for generations.

This declaration further intrigued me and I asked Harry and Jimmy if I could see their father dowse for water sometime.

I got my chance to witness vining firsthand early one summer morning after my friends invited me to watch their father dowse for a well on one of our neighbor's properties.

I was very excited about the chance to learn about vining and immediately rushed into my house to ask my grandmother for permission to watch Mr. Smith in action. My grandmother gladly granted me permission to go water witching with my friends and their dad. She also told me, "It will be good for you to get acquainted with some of the old ways and to respect and obey Mr. Smith at all times." I promised to respect her wishes then rushed out to tell Harry and Jimmy the good news.

My expectant friends greeted me and were glad when I told them I could go dowsing with them. We then excitedly hopped on our bikes and pedaled as fast as we were able to meet their father.

The three of us got to the Smith's driveway in time to meet my friend's dad as he loaded a few carefully selected willow branches into his station wagon. These branches were freshly cut from a tree in the Smith's back yard and trimmed into the shape of a Y. Harry, Jimmy and I stood impatiently waiting to board our conveyance. As we nervously fidgeted My friend's father looked at me and solemnly stated, "So you want to learn to find water?"

I shyly nodded. He smiled then patted me on the back and we were off.

My friends and I sat quietly as we rode to our destination. While we journeyed, Mr. Smith educated me about the importance of vining and told me that only a few gifted people could locate water using this very old method. I soon realized dowsing was a genuine folkway and not a foolish amusement.

We arrived at our destination, a dairy farm owned by a man named Brown, in no time. Mr. Smith carefully parked his car next to the Brown's barn, then sternly told my friends and me to keep quiet and stay out of the way. We obeyed and distanced ourselves then attentively observed our neighborhood dowser achieve his feat of wonder.

Mr. Smith first retrieved one of the flexible willow branches he had previously placed under some damp burlap in the back of his car. He then grasped the bough by the tips of its two narrowest and most limber offshoots thereby leaving the broad stem of the branch to be utilized as a pointer to indicate the location of water. He next held the willow branch so that it was oriented vertically and pointed to the sky. Subsequently Mr. Smith walked his client's pasture in a systematic manner until the tip of his dowsing rod moved and pointed directly at the ground. He then re-positioned the pointer of his branched instrument skyward and successfully dowsed the same piece of ground from several different directions until he was sure he located water.

After successfully completing this time honored and curious practice, my friend's father stated, "Its right here and 40 feet down."

Mr. Brown immediately positioned his tractor and began to dig. I was awe struck later that afternoon when the dairyman struck water in the exact location and at the same depth our local dowser had indicated earlier.

I went on several other successful vining expeditions with my friends. I was always astonished by the simplistic and unscientific method Mr. Smith employed to find water. As time passed, I came to welcome vining as bona fide folkway with a long history and an enduring cultural purpose to the Oregonian lifestyle of my youth.

Planting by the moon was another folkway I came upon as a child growing up with my grandparents. This agricultural tradition can be traced back to both the ancient Egyptian and Babylonian cultures as a method for assuring successful crop yields. Planting by the moon has continued as a favored agricultural practice through the millennia and was traditionally employed by many of the farming families who lived in the rural surroundings of my childhood.

My grandfather introduced me to moon planting early one spring when I was very young. My grampa told me about the four types of plants to grow as food – root crops, foliage crops, crops with external seeds and crops with internal seeds. He told me about the moon's cycle of 29.6 days and how that cycle was divided into four phases, with each phase being particularly suitable to one of the four previously stated crop types. However, the one central concept he stressed most was that his planting wasn't controlled by the moon or the weather but by God, who controlled the moon and the weather.

My grandfather's traditional belief in planting by the moon was confirmed to me in two ways — consistency and volume. First, I observed the unfailing success of moon planting through the consistent and successful crop yields our garden produced year after year. Second, I noted the crop yields of the gardens whose families practiced moon planting were significantly higher as opposed to the families who did not follow the edicts of that ancient folkway.

As time passed, I began to first consider then value this lunar method of planting crops, not only for its history but for its effectiveness. Slowly, I came to realize planting by the moon was another legitimate cultural tradition widely practiced by many who lived in my rural locality and ultimately appreciated as a valuable folkway critical to the society of my early life.

Moon shining was a very interesting folkway I encountered during my formative years in southern Oregon. There were countless times when I helped my friends to either work on their Dad's stills or prepare the recipes for their father's respective moonshine operations.

Moon shining involved the illegal manufacture of a highly potent form of booze that was known in my neighborhood as moonshine, white lightning or mountain dew. This intoxicating beverage was considered a highly valuable commodity in the rural surroundings of my youth.

Several local families produced white lightning for their personal recreational purposes or traded the potion on the local underground market. I found moon shining interesting because of its history, popularity as well as its odd and involved method of production.

The history of American moonshine can be traced back to the first settlers who arrived in Appalachia during the early half of the 1700's. That immigration included large numbers of Scotch-Irish and English frontiersmen who included the production of homemade whiskey as a mainstay to their way of life. As the numbers of those Gaelic frontiersmen steadily grew the popularity of their distilled beverage increased while eighteenth and nineteenth century America evolved.

The practice of making moon shine arrived in the Rogue Valley with the early settlers who first traveled to Oregon during the early half of the nineteenth century. Later, when prohibition was enacted under the Eighteenth Amendment, moon shining gained enormous popularity as a method to provide inebriating alcohol to people in need. As time went on, the Eighteenth Amendment was repealed and moon shining remained popular as a limited cultural endeavor of southern Oregon to this day.

Mountain dew was a very well-liked beverage in the pastoral environs where I grew up. Many of our local men preferred moonshine to beer and quaffed the hard potion regularly. Several of the patriarchs of my neighborhood owned stills and produced their own form of white lightning from their treasured family recipes. This prized potion was frequently bargained for goods and services or presented as a gift.

Often my grandfather was presented jars of mountain dew as payment for some act of good will. My grampa always welcomed those valued distilled offerings for their properties as a quality weed killer or suitable substitute for his lawn mower fuel.

Making moon shine is not a simple process and requires skill and practice to produce a desired product. There are two things every moon shiner should have if he or she is to be successful — a recipe and a still. The recipe required to produce mountain dew consists of the ingredients and their quantities blended to concoct the mash. The still is the primary piece of equipment used to produce moon shine via cooking the mash to eventually derive potable alcohol.

There are hundreds of moonshine recipes, each containing varied ingredients of differing quantity. The recipe commonly utilized in my old neighborhood was called a corn mash recipe. This recipe included 10 gallons of water, 17 pounds of corn kernels, 3 pounds of malted barley and 3 ounces of yeast. These ingredients were first mixed, well stirred, left to ferment for one to two weeks then finally placed in a pre-heated still for distillation. The mash was subsequently cooked until a condensed highly alcoholic residue was rendered. The volumetric yield from this recipe was low but ample for household consumption.

Moonshine stills, like moon shine recipes, vary in type and size. The type of still used for moon shining in my locale was called a thumper still. These stills were named after one of its components, the thumper keg. Our thumper stills were homemade from copper and a variety of salvaged components that required time and skilled effort to construct.

Basically, there were four parts associated with our thumper stills, each interconnected via copper tubing. The main parts of our stills were first soldered together, Next, these soldered sections were snug fitted and sealed with an oatmeal paste to the other components of those homemade distilling contraptions.

The first component of our still was named the cooking pot and was utilized via open flame to heat the mash and produce an alcohol laden vapor which was in turn transferred to the second component of our still.

The second component to our distilling device was called the thumper keg and served as the first filter for the hot alcohol vapors that were transferred from the cooking pot. The name thumper keg was derived from the thumping sound emitted as the pressurized mash particles separated from the transferred alcoholic vapors emitted from the cooking pot and settled to the bottom of the thumper barrel.

The worm keg was the third component utilized in our homemade stills. The worm keg trapped and condensed the alcohol vapors transferred from the thumper keg to create a highly potent beverage.

This part of the still was named for its long, winding coil immersed in the cool water that filled the worm keg.

The fourth component of our thumper still was the catch bucket. This part was loosely fitted to the end of the worm coil located on the outside of the lower section of the worm keg. The catch bucket was always filled with cotton or some type of fabric and was utilized as a final filter for the potent mountain dew.

Once a suitable quantity of mountain dew had been produced, it was tested for proof. There were several ways to test the efficacy of moonshine ranging from igniting the fluid and looking for the desirable blue flame to using a hydrometer.

The moonshine test method used by the men in my old neighborhood was the bubble test. This test was conducted by taking capped jars partially filled with white lightning, then shaking the containers to see the size and the duration of the life of the created bubbles. A skilled moonshiner could accurately estimate the alcohol content of his product to within 20 to 30 proof of its actual alcohol value via this ingenious method of proof testing.

Moon shining was a folkway I found extremely interesting as I grew up in southern Oregon. I learned the historical import assigned to moon shining as I witnessed the men of my neighborhood talk of their family's long association with the production of white lightning. As time passed, I realized the popularity as well as the cultural influence of moonshine via the consistent prized value associated with its creation. I still recall the first time I saw a functioning moon shine still with its gleaming copper and brass components so mysterious and wondrous to my eight year old mind.

The history, popularity and ingenious instrumentalities associated with the production of mountain dew have always intrigued me. I truly feel moon shining should be regarded as a folkway due to the strong position this activity held within the culture of my rural Oregonian upbringing.

Folk medicine was the final influential folkway of my rustic cultural background. Folk medicine, also known as traditional medicine, alternative medicine or natural medicine, has been practiced since prehistoric times and continues as an art of healing today. The ancient Egyptians practiced their version of traditional medicine over 50 centuries ago. Folk medicine was also practiced in ancient Greece and within the Roman Empire.

As the centuries passed and Western Civilization advanced, the treatments and remedies associated with natural medicine continued to develop. The concept of manifest destiny served folk medicine well, seeing this folkway maintain it's vital role within the construct of American settlement.

Some herbal medications and treatments associated with alternative medicine have been used in Oregon since the first Native Americans arrived. A few early Native American cures have continued in popularity and with the passage of time, have been blended via cultural contact with the imported old world herbal cures of the frontier settlers. Many of these hybridized natural medicines are currently utilized and remain essential to the wellbeing of those now dwelling in the Rogue Valley.

The folk medicines and treatments I recall each have extensive histories and include the use of herbs such as ginseng, honey and honeysuckle. These substances can be employed in a variety of ingenious ways including pastes, teas, and tonics or mixed as lotions for treatments to the skin. Poultices were also widely used as therapies to treat medicinal problems. These moist preparations were adapted to counteract a plethora of problems associated with injury or sickness.

Ginseng has long been valued for its medicinal quality by a variety of cultures up to the present day. The Chinese have recognized the restorative properties of ginseng for thousands of years. Chinese folk medicine practitioners still believe ginseng is an effective stimulant to increase personal vitality, invigorate the mind and increase sexual performance. Native American people also utilized ginseng as a medication to treat various forms of fatigue. In the northwest, this herb has been readily prescribed by Oregonian herbalists, mothers and wives, to enhance their patient's energy and strength for over one hundred years. In recent years, ginseng has become highly valuable and is not only sought on public land but grown on private property for profit throughout Oregon, Washington and Idaho.

The ladies of Elliott Road readily utilized ginseng as a medicinal aid for nervousness, fatigue or loss of strength. My Grandmother consistently brewed ginseng tea for my grandfather when he was feeling stressed or tired and he always said he felt better after quaffing a cup the warm herbal beverage.

Honey was another popular folk medicine employed by the families I grew up with in rural southern Oregon.

This versatile golden substance has been successfully utilized by man for thousands of years in a variety of ways and is still found to be of value today. The medicinal usefulness of honey was first mentioned by the ancient Egyptians in a text labeled the Smith Papyrus. These early people utilized the viscous material as an agent to fight infection. Later, the curative value of honey was realized by the Greeks and Romans, who employed this amber fluid with a purpose similar to their earlier Egyptian counterparts. The therapeutic usefulness of honey continued while Western Civilization advanced. American colonists and settlers consistently relied on the beneficial properties of the tawny substance to address their medicinal and culinary needs as they traveled westward.

Native Americans in the Rogue River valley were culturally unfamiliar with the medicinal benefits of honey. However, these ingenious people readily utilized bee pollen to supplement their medicinal needs.

Honey was first made available in southern Oregon by the early settlers from the east who established themselves in the mid 1800's. Since then, the golden ambrosia has continued to be favored by people living in the Rogue Valley for its time tested usefulness as a medicine and a sweetener.

The mothers and wives of my old neighborhood continually recognized the healing properties of honey and used it as the initial form of first aid for the successful treatment of burns and infections. My grandmother always had a jar of honey in her medicine cabinet and readily applied the viscous amber material to the point of injury whenever I had a scrape, cut or burn.

I favored this folk remedy not only for its medicinal effectiveness but for its sweet taste.

Honeysuckle was yet another folk medicine recognized by the individuals and families of my pastoral childhood. This sweet smelling flower was primarily used to treat a variety of skin ailments and usually was administered as a key ingredient in oils, lotions or emulsions.

The honeysuckle plant has a long and impressive history for the treatment of a variety of ailments within many cultures.

The medicinal usefulness of honeysuckle can be traced to the era of the Ancient Roman Empire where it was recommended as a useful medication to treat maladies of the spleen. Seventh century Chinese herbalists recommended honeysuckle as a curative to purge toxins from the body. Native Americans relied on honeysuckle as a remedy for bee stings, asthma and sore throats. In the middle ages, people utilized the fragrant bloom to treat rashes, sores, tumors and various skin diseases.

As time passed, the medicinal efficacy of honeysuckle was not forgotten. The therapeutic value of this plant remained as a vital component of frontier medicine while western civilization progressed and the settlement of America evolved.

The herbal usefulness of honeysuckle was realized by the early settlers of Oregon who steadily made their way into the Rogue River Valley during the early part of the nineteenth century. As the years marched on, the effectiveness of this sweet smelling bloom continued to be recognized and prescribed by Oregonian herbalists for the treatment of skin problems.

My grandmother consistently grew and harvested honeysuckle to use as an ingredient in an appealing curative liquid she created to treat for sunburn, bee stings and rashes. We called my gramma's sweet smelling potion her sweet oil and I can personally testify to its effectiveness.

Countless times I rushed to my matriarch to care for a skin problem I encountered and countless times she cured my dermal injuries with her fragrant emulsion.

Herbal poultices were the last of the country medications I recall from the time I spent growing up in pastoral southern Oregon. Those medicinal compresses were a very effective folk medicine and remain as a popular remedy for a variety of wounds today.

A poultice consists of a bandage treated with a desired substance that has been rendered to a soft, moist, medicinal paste. This therapeutic dressing is first placed, then bandaged directly over a freshly washed cut, sore, abrasion or aching part of the person undergoing treatment. The curative placement of the poultice allows the healing properties of the medicinal paste to be absorbed into the wound while the compress draws the harmful agents away from the point of injury and into the bandage.

The history associated with poultices is long as well as varied. These medicinal compresses have been created from a variety of recipes and have been utilized over thousands of years by many societies. Ancient Egyptians, ancient Greeks, Romans, Europeans and Native Americans each utilized poultices as part of their medicinal regimen.

Ancient Egypt's use of poultices can be traced back to the second intermediate period of that nation's history, (circa 1600 B.C.) The early Egyptians utilized the leaves of the willow, sycamore, acacia, honey, and a variety of other ingredients in their medicinal compresses for treating a plethora of wounds and injuries.

The Classic Greek association with poultices goes back to the time of Homer, (circa 800 B.C.) and probably farther.

The ancient poet wrote of the type of poultice used in the treatment of festering battle wounds.

The Romans were also familiar with the use of herbal compresses to cure battlefield cuts, burns or abrasions. The word poultice is derived from the Latin puls or pultes, meaning porridge.

As the history of western civilization advanced, a consistent body of evidence arose to attest of the continued use of poultices as a valued medicinal practice. The therapeutic compresses were constantly utilized as a successful treatment for a variety of ailments throughout Europe during the middle ages, the renaissance and on to the period of American colonization.

The first colonists who arrived in America were very familiar with the medicinal value of poultices. As the American frontier expanded westward, pioneers and the medical practitioners who settled the land gained an extensive knowledge of the indigenous plants from the Native American people. This priceless information was utilized in the creation of new indigenous poultice recipes. Those new recipes proved to be increasingly gainful to the therapeutic efforts of the pioneer medicinal practitioners and caregivers who settled the American west.

As time passed, herbalists, country doctors and individuals began to settle the Rogue Valley. Those Oregonian frontier physicians and caregivers continued to rely on poultices as a vital component of their medicinal regimen.

As Oregon grew, the medicinal usefulness of poultices was passed down from generation to generation to continue as a popular healing therapy into the modern era. Today many Oregonian herbalists, doctors, caregivers and mothers rely on poultices as an effective and proven remedy for the treatment of a variety of ailments and wounds.

The use of poultices was part of the folk medicine my grandmother relied on as an essential component of her household first aid kit. My gramma consistently utilized a lard and salt poultice therapy to remedy the frequent wounds I incurred during my youth.

Her compresses never failed and usually produced a complete recovery in one to two days. The history, popularity and medicinal effectiveness associated with this folk medicine position poultices as a medicinal folkway of the Rogue River Valley.

The extensive chronicle, esteem and therapeutic usefulness connected to the ginseng, honey, honeysuckle and poultice remedies of my grandmother evidenced the cultural importance of folk medicine to me. As I grew to manhood, I learned to respect folk medicine as a useful, time honored and popular practice so much a part of the cultural tapestry I fondly recall of my childhood home. The Folkways I encountered as a Southern Oregonian boy growing up were wonderful as well as educational.

I am truly grateful for the opportunity of being exposed to those traditional customs during those formative years of my Southern Oregonian youth.

Epilogue

The life I had growing up in rural Southern Oregon was magnificent. My family, my friends, my experiences, and my pets all were vital to the development of what I have become. My journey's during those golden days of childhood remain as bastions of wholesomeness and pleasure within my mind.

Made in the USA
San Bernardino, CA
28 October 2016